*To Bernard + Sylvia with all best wishes from John. " Oct 02.*

# Pooh
## and the
# Psychologists

Winnie-the-Pooh, in his nurturing role, solves the problems of his friends and effectively brings changes to their lives. John Tyerman Williams discovers that Pooh, with the breadth of his psychological knowledge and his skill in applying it, proves himself to be a brilliant psychotherapist.

John Tyerman Williams is a Doctor of Philosophy at Oxford University and lectures on theatre, English literature and English history. He is married to psychologist Dr Elizabeth Mapstone and lives in Cornwall.

*'I have enjoyed this little book . . . tremendously – and to my mind it is the most successful of the three.'*

ANDREW ROBSON ON THE INTERNET

*'...recommended reading for all students and practitioners in the helping metier.'*

DR HALLA BELOFF IN *THE PSYCHOLOGIST*

D1148651

*Also by John Tyerman Williams*

POOH AND THE PHILOSOPHERS
POOH AND THE SECOND MILLENNIUM
(*A paperback edition of Pooh and the Ancient Mysteries*)

JOHN TYERMAN WILLIAMS

# *Pooh*
## *and the*
# *Psychologists*

*With illustrations by*
*Ernest H. Shepard*

EGMONT

First published in hardback in Great Britain 2000
printed under the Methuen imprint
This paperback edition first published 2002
By Egmont Books Limited
239 Kensington High Street
London W8 6SA

Copyright © 2000 John Tyerman Williams
The author has asserted his moral rights

Texts by A.A.Milne and line illustrations by E.H.Shepard
from *Winnie-the-Pooh* and *The House at Pooh Corner*
copyright under the Berne Convention
Grateful acknowledgement is made to the Trustees of the Pooh Properties
for the use of the quoted material by A.A. Milne and the illustrations by E.H. Shepard

Cover illustrations by Mark Burgess
Copyright © 2000 Egmont Books Limited

A CIP catalogue record for this title
is available from the British Library

ISBN 0 416 20044 3

1 3 5 7 9 10 8 6 4 2

Printed and bound in Great Britain

This book is sold subject to the condition that it shall not, by way of
trade or otherwise, be lent, resold, hired out, or otherwise circulated
without the publisher's prior consent in any form of binding or cover
other than that in which it is published and without a similar condition
including this condition being imposed on the subsequent purchaser.

To Dr Elizabeth Mapstone,
*a psychologist*
*whom Pooh would be proud to salute*

## Acknowledgements

My chief, and enormous, debt is to Dr Elizabeth Mapstone, who gave, not only her usual encouragement and constructive criticism, but also her professional expertise as a psychologist. This guided me *to* much valuable information and *away* from many errors. Any remaining errors are my own. So, of course, are the interpretations.

I should also like to thank Susan Hitches, my Senior Editor, who was most pleasant and helpful to work with; Vanessa Mitchell, my Desk Editor, who clarified the text in several places, and Mark Burgess, for his attractive cover design.

# Contents

## Introducing Winnie-the-Pooh
## super - psychologist

'One must recognize the central position of
Winnie-the-Pooh.' *Playing and Reality*

This was the opinion of D. W. Winnicott (1896–1971),
perhaps the most eminent English child psychologist of
his time and a one-time President of the British Psycho-
Analytical Society. It is humbling to find it took a
psycho-analyst, even a major one, to point towards an
important truth undiscovered by professed Ursinologists:
the truth that Winnie-the-Pooh is a master of
psychology. However, the humility proper to (though not
always found in) the scientific investigator should lead us
to welcome Winnicott's insight: an insight which inspired
me to investigate a hitherto neglected area of the
Enormous Brain of Winnie-the-Pooh.

Winnicott was emphasizing the importance of the teddy
bear in a child's development. But there is far more to
Pooh's 'central position' than this. Pooh was a major
psychologist in his own right, and one who took an *active*

role in solving the psychological problems of his friends. The pleasant task of this little introductory work is to demonstrate beyond all reasonable doubt that Pooh Bear is indeed a super-psychologist and a brilliant psycho-therapist.

I have chosen to present a series of case studies which unmistakably demonstrate his therapeutic powers. This approach has the advantage of renewing our acquaintance with Pooh's friends and casting a fresh light on them, while providing ample evidence of the wide-ranging theoretical knowledge that underpinned Pooh's practical skills.

All serious Ursinologists must have noticed important changes in the personalities of some of Pooh Bear's friends. The timid and over-dependent Piglet is transformed into the hero who rescues Wol and even Pooh himself. Rabbit becomes less bossy and drops his original xenophobic prejudice against newcomers like Kanga and Tigger. The once solitary and depressive Eeyore becomes actively helpful and ends up living a more social life.

Careful readers must have asked themselves what caused these remarkable changes. The answer, of course, is Winnie-the-Pooh himself. He is the super-therapist who worked the cures. Given this clue, we shall not be surprised to find that the Enormous Brain of Pooh contained complete knowledge of a wide variety of psychological theories and practices, including those labelled behaviourist, cognitive, analytical, developmental, humanistic, social and psycholinguistic. He had complete mastery, in fact, of everything that was relevant to the problems of his friends, whom he treated so unobtrusively yet so effectively. He was even familiar with the esoteric realm of Buddhist psychology, with its emphasis on personal experience, and on the inevitable element of emotion in perception. This wide-ranging knowledge, when joined to his superlative judgement, enabled him always to choose the approach, or combination of approaches, best suited to each particular case.

Here some readers well acquainted with the history of psychology may raise an objection. How, they may ask, could Winnie-the-Pooh, whose contributions to this subject were published between 1924 (*When We Were Very Young*) and 1928 (*The House at Pooh Corner*) show knowledge of, for example, cognitive psychology, which developed from the 1950s, of Jaques Lacan, whose distinctive approach to psycho-analysis appeared in the same decade, or of evolutionary psychology, which has emerged only in the last quarter of this century?

The answer, of course, is that one aspect of the Great Bear's genius is his frequent anticipation of theories and practices which more plodding psychologists arrived at much later.

His openness to all kinds of theory and his flexibility in applying them is another example of his being ahead of his time. In the early part of the twentieth century, psychologists tended to be narrowly sectarian. Behaviourists despised the analytical schools, while analysts not only reciprocated this contempt but were themselves fiercely divided between Freudians, Jungians and Adlerians. In the latter part of the century, there was growing appreciation of other schools. As early as the 1960s, psychologists praised Gordon Allport (1897–1967) for 'a discriminating eclecticism'. Roger Brown and Richard J. Herrnstein's much admired textbook *Psychology* says, 'Most psychologists are not adherents of schools but are theoretical eclectics who use different concepts for different phenomena.' It is gratifying to Ursinologists to see Pooh's eminent successors catching up with him.

In addition to demonstrating his mastery of all known psychology, Pooh Bear made two remarkable independent contributions to psychotherapeutic technique: (i) his use of patients' own freely chosen and totally independent activities as therapy; (ii) his personal demonstration of certain problems and different methods of treating them.

The first pervades the whole of his therapeutic work. It is a major factor in his ability to act as a psychotherapist without ever presenting himself overtly and officially in that role. That remarkable existential psychiatrist R. D. Laing (1927–1989) complained that conventional therapeutic conditions set up artificial barriers between therapist and client. Pooh's approach anticipated and avoided this difficulty.

His second contribution is an even more remarkable example of his innovative technique. Perhaps for this reason, we find an example of it early in the Pooh casebook.

## Pooh on eating problems

Even the most superficial of Ursinologists must remember the occasion when Winnie-the-Pooh visited Rabbit and enjoyed Rabbit's hospitality so enthusiastically that he could not get out through Rabbit's door and became 'a Wedged Bear in Great Tightness'. As a result, he had to stay there without food for a week until he had slimmed enough to be pulled to freedom.

It is painful to record that this incident has often been cited as the strongest evidence that Pooh was greedy. The exact opposite is the case. Pooh was in fact typically sacrificing his own dignity and comfort to teaching his friends and succeeding generations a most valuable lesson. His plight as a Wedged Bear warned us all of the dangers of over-eating. Ursinologists may go on to interpret this this as an example of aversion therapy, a form of Behavioural therapy where a bad habit is cured by connecting it with unpleasant consequences. This treatment is particularly associated with the Behaviourism of B. F. Skinner (1904–1990).

While these scholars are certainly correct in dismissing the notion that Pooh was greedy, the rest of their judgement is seriously flawed. Though aversion therapy was at one time practised with high hopes of success, it is now generally regarded as a failure, at least so far as long-term results are concerned. People who want to give up smoking, for example, usually do so while they are actually undergoing aversion therapy but frequently revert after the treatment ceases.

It is obviously unthinkable that Pooh was unaware of this. Indeed, his subsequent behaviour shows this quite clearly. Far from being put off honey by this experience, he continues undeterred to indulge his taste for it. Always, of course, in strictly moderate quantities, as the repeated terms 'a *little* something' (my italics) and a 'smackerel' testify.

What then was his true purpose in this demonstration? At least three answers leap to mind.

1. The obvious purpose was to warn others of the potentially painful results of over-eating.
2. More convincingly – and perhaps ahead of his time – to point out that extreme and harsh interventions were unlikely to produce lasting benefit.

3. Most prophetic of all, here and throughout the two volumes, he warned us against an unbalanced passion for slimness, a warning which we can appreciate better today when anorexia nervosa and bulimia are such present dangers. Pooh, as 'a Stout and Helpful Bear' is a lasting reminder that mental and bodily health can go together with a pleasing, though never an excessive, plumpness.

## Milne plants the clue

Once Winnicott has alerted us to the psychological domain of Pooh, we merely have to look for the relevant clues. As always, Milne has planted them with scrupulous fairness. If, then, these clues are planted so fairly, some may ask why nobody has picked them up before? It is a pleasure to give an answer that redounds to the credit both of the author and of his earlier readers. The surface meaning of the Pooh saga provides such complete satisfaction that it might well seem greedy to look for more. Nevertheless, it would be a sad loss to humanity if the deeper levels of Milnean meaning were not mined and brought to the surface.

The first clue to the psychological level of our texts lies in the Introduction to *Winnie-the-Pooh*. Here we meet the problem of 'whether twice seven is twelve or twenty-two'. It is obvious to any competent Ursinologist that the apparent problem cannot be the real one. In 'Us Two' (*Now We Are Six*), Christopher Robin and Pooh agree that twenty-two is the product of twice eleven. We know also that Christopher Robin was able to try teaching the 'Twy-Stymes' table to Winnie-the-Pooh. It follows that he could not have any serious doubt about twice seven. What, then, is the true interpretation of this little arithmetical problem?

I felt it natural to seek the explanation from the father of psycho-analysis himself, Sigmund Freud (1856–1939). And, as we are dealing with numbers, the relevant Freudian source is obviously the section on numbers in Chapter XII of *The Psychopathology of Everyday Life*, one of Freud's most popular works.

There Freud argues that if one takes any number, apparently at random, analysis will show that this number invariably has a vital connection with the chooser's mind. The connection may be buried deep in the unconscious, but it is always there.

In case what follows may seem a trifle far-fetched, I assure my readers that it is considerably simpler than some of Freud's own examples, which often depend on quite complex (unconscious) mental arithmetic. Examining Milne's figures, I saw 2 7 12 22. After a good deal of experiment, I reached the following answer: $2 (7+12. 22)$, which produced $2 (1922)$.

The meaning was now clear. For our special dedication to Pooh must never make us forget that Milne was a highly successful author in several genres. As well as being a successful journalist and dramatist, he wrote an excellent detective novel, *The Red House Mystery*, published in – of course: 1922. Where could a clue be planted more appropriately than in the date of a detective story? And what could be more appropriate than an application of Freudian numerology as a pointer to Ursinological psychology?

To establish the meaning beyond all reasonable doubt, the figure 2 in the product tells us that we must look for two sources. The obvious interpretation leads us to *Winnie-the-Pooh* and *The House at Pooh Corner*. Another interpretation will suggest we look for two kinds of source: the verse of *When We Were Very Young* and *Now We Are Six*, as well as the two prose works. We shall soon find good reason for accepting this wider interpretation

## Pooh's professional status

Some professional psychologists may feel I am using the term 'psychology' too loosely. I hope that later passages will assure them that I recognize the important differences between, for example, psycho-analysts, psychiatrists and psychologists in the narrower sense. But when I talk of Pooh and the psychologists, I am following *Chambers 21st Century Dictionary*, which defines psychology as 'the study of mind and behaviour' and William James's classic definition, 'the Science of Mental Life', a definition repeated with a caveat by Professor George Miller in 1962. Miller's caveat emphasizes that the concept of a science of mental life has grown more complex and difficult to define since James's day. Happily, the Great Bear was well aware of this nearly half a century earlier than Miller.

Readers will rightly expect me to justify the large claims I make for the breadth of Pooh's psychological knowledge and his therapeutic skill in applying it. I am modestly confident that the wealth of material in the Milnean texts will enable me to satisfy all rational demands. Of course, though, that very wealth cannot be exhausted. Selection is inevitable, both in the examples studied and the interpretations suggested. In all my Ursinological studies, I have hoped to stimulate my readers to make their own researches and – even more – to reach their own interpretations. The following little introductory work should give them ample opportunities to do both.

I should now like to suggest a problem here and now. Early in the very first of the Pooh case studies, we read that 'Winnie-the-Pooh lived in a forest all by himself under the name of Sanders', and that he had the name over the door in gold letters. Why 'Sanders'? And why gold letters? Winnie-the-Pooh is referred to by several different forms of his name, but never again as 'Sanders'. Yet we cannot dismiss this as a trivial matter. Every word in the Milnean text is chosen with an accuracy that Flaubert might have envied. Its importance is emphasized because it is part of our first impression of Pooh. Moreover, it exists pictorially as well as verbally. Perhaps Shepard's illustration will provide a clue. Let us examine it.

The picture adds at least two pieces of obviously relevant information. The name 'Sanders' is prefixed by a title, and the title is partly hidden by a doorbell. What are we to make of these undoubtedly crucial facts?

Though the second letter of the title is clearly 'r', the first looks like 'M', which would give us the conventional 'Mr'. This is confirmed in two of the later pictures. Now 'Mr' often distinguishes a specialist from the 'Dr' of a general practioner. In that case, might not the gold letters stand for the more usual brass plate of a professional, or, in this case, a psychotherapist? And then the bell's function would be to inform Pooh that a patient was waiting his attention.

How does 'Sanders' fit in with this hypothesis?

Remembering that our present studies were inspired by the great child psychologist D. W. Winnicot, we also remember that sleepy children are often told the sandman is coming. As Winnicott was also a psycho-analyst, thinking of sleep inevitably leads to thinking of dreams, a main source of material for analysts of all schools. Nor was this connection known only to psychotherapists: some years ago, a popular song contained the line 'Oh, Mr Sandman, send me a dream'. Taking all these facts together, may we not interpret them as telling us to be aware of Pooh as psychologist and so perhaps an interpreter of dreams?

Before answering this question, let us heed the advice given by that enthusiastic interpreter of dreams, Freud himself. He wrote that it is 'the stricter method of verification and the striving for far-reaching connections which make up the essential character of scientific work'. Unless we apply rigorous verification, we may find ourselves making connections not so much far-reaching as far-fetched. As we go on, my readers will see how carefully I heed this warning.

## Case 1

### Pooh cures Christopher Robin's Arktophobia

Near the beginning of *When We Were Very Young* we find the poem 'Lines and Squares', which begins

> Whenever I walk in a London street,
> I'm ever so careful to watch my feet;
> And I keep in the squares,
> And the masses of bears,
> Who wait at the corners all ready to eat
> The sillies who tread on the lines of the street,
> Go back to their lairs,
> And I say to them, "Bears,
> Just look how I'm walking in all the squares!"

Here we have a marked case of Arktophobia (an irrational fear of bears). So severe is Christopher Robin's Arktophobia at this stage that he dismisses those who do not share it as 'sillies'. This is in the sharpest possible contrast to his attitude throughout the prose Pooh saga. An irrational fear of bears has been replaced by a warm

13

and unclouded friendship with the Great Bear. Indeed, we may feel that the cure has gone a little too far. Christopher Robin's attitude to Pooh is affectionate but usually somewhat patronizing. Only once – in the matter of naming the rescue vessel *The Brain of Pooh* (see *Winnie-the-Pooh*, Chapter Nine: 'In which Piglet is entirely surrounded by water') – does he show the slightest glimmering of recognition that he is in the presence of an Enormous Brain. Whatever we may feel about that, we cannot doubt that Christopher Robin's Arktophobia has been effectively cured. This raises the question: How?

Like the morbid condition, the therapy adopted is clearly laid out in the two volumes of poetry. Towards the end of *When We Were Very Young* comes the poem 'Teddy Bear'. The title alone is enough to attract any Ursinologist. Moreover, this poem's special importance is signalled by its being by far the longest in this collection. At first sight, the subject is unmistakably a teddy bear in the sense of a nursery toy. Even this is a marked step forward. The bear is no longer an imaginary enemy but a familiar toy, regarded no longer with fear but with affection.

A complete analysis of this key text would take up too much space in an introductory study like this. So would even a detailed comparison of Teddy with Winnie-the-Pooh. Before continuing with this case history of Arktophobia, though, I must call my readers' attention to a few salient facts which should stimulate further thought:

1. At first, Teddy appears purely passive. He falls off the ottoman, 'But generally seems to lack/The energy to clamber back.' (Surely a euphemism for 'cannot'.)
2. Yet later he is clearly capable of independent movement. E. H. Shepard shows him standing up and looking at his reflection in a cheval-glass. Near the end,

he goes down into the street to ask the plump man if he is the King of France, and we see him bowing to the King.

3. Even more remarkable is his motive for all this. He has become worried because he is so stout. He is partly consoled when he reads that a distinctly 'stoutish' King of France was 'Nicknamed "The Handsome"'. His contentment is confirmed when he meets 'This man of

adiposity' who agrees that he is the King of France.

4. This little episode reveals that Teddy is capable of self-consciousness and anxiety.

5. He is also literate. He *reads* (my emphasis) about the Handsome King of France. He corrects 'as fat as me' to 'as fat as I': a correction which our laxer age might consider verging on the pedantic.

6. Finally, this bear is usually referred to as 'Teddy' or 'Teddy Bear'. Just twice, and then during his colloquy with the King of France, he is called 'Mr Edward Bear'. Now the word 'Teddy' never occurs in the two major Milnean texts.

But even the most casual reader must remember that the very first paragraph of Chapter One begins 'Here is

Edward Bear . . .' That paragraph ends 'Anyhow, here he is ready to be introduced to you. Winnie-the-Pooh.' This change of name clearly indicates the transition from a much loved nursery toy to the Enormous Brain of Pooh, to whose psychological skills we now return.

All Ursinologists who are also familiar with the techniques of Behavioural Psychology will have realized already that we are looking at what is called 'systematic desensitization'. This is a form of deconditioning in which a step by step approach eventually enables the client to face the former fear in a relaxed and confident manner. By the

end of *When We Were Very Young*, Christopher Robin has moved from fear of bears to sharing his nursery first with a toy teddy bear and then with a living bear.

We see this process continue in *Now We Are Six*. In 'Us Two', Christopher Robin has formed a special bond with his bear; significantly now called 'Pooh'. In 'Furry Bear', a recognizably Pooh-type bear is looking at a bigger black bear in a cage. By now, it is only the friendly bear who is free. The potentially dangerous bear is safely barred away. So, in 'Waiting at the Window', Christopher Robin can concentrate on the race between two rain drops, not even needing to notice the bear who shares his window seat.

Finally, illustrating the poem 'The End', we see a picture of Christopher Robin dancing happily with his bear and Piglet, a picture echoing the recent masterpiece, *Winnie-the-Pooh*.

Having satisfactorily demonstrated the success of the cure and the kind of therapy used, I must now fulfil my promise to identify Winnie-the-Pooh as the therapist who effected the cure. No doubt many of my readers will have picked up the necessary clues themselves, but I feel the train of evidence should be made explicit. So I will outline the succession of roles played by Winnie-the-Pooh as therapist. These roles come gradually closer to revealing his true nature, though the complete revelation is reserved for the prose works.

This is one of the many occasions on which the evidence of E. H. Shepard's illustrations is vital. At each stage of Christopher Robin's progress, we find pictures of a bear, visually indistinguishable from Pooh Bear himself. The plain words of the text, however, seem to forbid identification. The poem 'Teddy Bear', for example, tells us that Teddy lacks exercise, whereas we all know that Pooh does regular stoutness exercises and takes frequent walks in every kind of weather.

In 'Us Two', the bear is no longer regarded as a mere nursery toy; he is actually called 'Pooh', though not, interestingly, 'Winnie-the-Pooh', still less, 'Winnie-*ther*-Pooh'. We notice that he not only builds up Christopher Robin's intellectual confidence by constantly corroborating his ideas, but also his courage by saying, 'I'm *never* afraid with you.' It would be obviously absurd to take literally this suggestion that the therapist needed protection by his client. What we see here is an early example of Pooh's willingness to assume a subordinate role in order to benefit his client. This beneficent humility is one of Pooh's characteristics, and one that distinguishes him from so many psychologists.

Before passing on to Pooh's next role, I must now call my reader's attention to a piece of evidence vital to understanding the nature of Pooh Bear. At the end of 'Us Two' we see a picture of Christopher Robin going upstairs, followed by Pooh, apparently to bed. To the shame of all Ursinologists, including, I must confess, me until this

moment, no one has previously pointed out the significance of the fact that Pooh is ascending the stairs by himself, unaided.

This at once solves the puzzle that has troubled many of us. At the beginning of *Winnie-the-Pooh*, we have the picture of him being bumped headfirst down the stairs and only dimly aware that there might be another way of coming down. Yet in the rest of the book we find him extremely active, even climbing trees. How do we reconcile these undisputed facts? Simply by realizing that, the text tells us, the bumping bear is Edward Bear, i.e., the nursery toy. The bear whose Enormous Brain we are privileged to study thereafter, is Winnie-*ther*-Pooh. Shepard's picture at the end of 'Us Two' confirms this hypothesis and also tells us that the 'Pooh' in that poem is approaching more closely to The Great Bear.

In 'Furry Bear', the Pooh-figure openly displays his mastery, while the furry bear is safely behind bars, yet, at the same time, he is presented as enviable in certain ways:

> If I were a bear,
>     And a big bear too,
> I shouldn't much care
>     If it froze or snew;
> I shouldn't much mind
>     If it snowed or friz –
> I'd be all fur-lined
>     With a coat like his!

'Waiting at the Window' brings the World of Pooh into focus. Below the window seat on which Christopher Robin and the bear are sitting, are clearly recognizable portraits of Piglet and Eeyore! And we have seen that 'The End', shows Christopher Robin dancing with – again recognizable – Pooh and Piglet. Thus, throughout the treatment of Christopher Robin's Arktophobia, a Pooh figure is always present. More importantly, as I demonstrated in the preceding pages, this Pooh figure grows ever more recognizable as Winnie-the-Pooh himself. Finally, then, we are left in no doubt that Pooh is the therapist who effected the cure.

Apart from the intrinsic interest of this case study, it shows how fairly Milne prepared his readers to look for psychological material in the two great prose works that followed. It also reminds us that we cannot fully appreciate those multi-layered masterpieces without careful study of their prolegomena – the introductory matter in the two verse collections. That this vital information has been discovered so belatedly gives rise to that truly scholarly combination of pained regret at the folly of others with a certain smugness about one's own superior wisdom.

The following chapters will show instances of Pooh's wide-ranging therapeutic skills and his faultless judgement in applying them. Some may feel that curing Christopher Robin's Arktophobia was an easy task. In fact, however, phobias can be extremely obstinate. Some unfortunate people, indeed, carry phobias learnt in childhood throughout their adult lives. It is true though that some of Pooh's cases did present him with greater challenges, culminating in his successful treatment of Eeyore's severe clinical depression; a condition both potentially crippling and notoriously resistant to treatment.

The desensitization therapy that we have watched Pooh use so successfully is a particular example of Behavioural therapy. It is difficult to define Behavioural therapy in a way that is neither too narrow nor too inclusive. It is enough to say here that Behavioural therapists believe that their patients' problems have been learned, and that the solutions can be learned, too, with proper therapeutic help.

Thus Christopher Robin feared bears, even in the most unlikely places. I think we are justified in assuming that he learned this fear. Such a fear and the belief in the magical protection of the squares could hardly be innate. It was a belief widely – though not seriously – held. Almost certainly some foolish or facetious elder implanted this fear in Christopher Robin's mind.

So, even before the major Pooh saga begins, Pooh had proved his claim to be a brilliantly effective

psychotherapist. Even more important for all lovers of Pooh, he had made the whole Pooh story possible. For if Christopher Robin had maintained his phobia about bears, there could have been no Winnie-the-Pooh. I would ask my readers to ponder this appalling possibility before reading on. Then I am sure they will approach the following case studies in the proper spirit of admiring gratitude to the great Bear.

## Case 2

### Pooh assists Piglet to mature

Piglet has a very special place in the world of Pooh. Right at the beginning, we read that the author says, 'My dear Piglet, the whole book is about you.' Looked at from this perspective, we can interpret the Milnean opus as the case study of how Piglet develops from the timid and emotionally dependent 'Very Small Animal' we first meet into the 'Brave' Piglet who rescues Wol and Pooh himself, and thus earns the supreme honour of being taken into Pooh's home just before the end of *The House at Pooh Corner.*

I have often complained of the extraordinary blindness of other scholars to the manifold meanings of the great Milnean texts. It is only honest therefore to confess that I too have been culpably blind to the obvious signals to

Piglet's progress that are placed, and placed prominently, at the beginning and the end of the Pooh saga.

We have often noticed the accolade Piglet receives near the end of *The House at Pooh Corner* when Pooh invites him to share his dwelling. But how many of us have connected this with the first appearance of Piglet? In the Introduction to *Winnie-the-Pooh*, we read 'Piglet is so small that he slips into a pocket'. The moment we put the two together the truth leaps at us from the printed page. Piglet's progress is summed up in his psychological growth from being in Christopher Robin's pocket to being in Winnie-the-Pooh's house.

Anyone who doubts the significance of this change has only to compare the situation of someone in the pocket of an amiable youth who has not yet grasped the twice times table with the situation of being in the house of Pooh, who, as I proved in *Pooh and the Philosophers*, is a master of Higher Mathematics, indeed of all Western philosophy, as well as being the Supreme Magus of the Second Millennium (see *Pooh and the Ancient Mysteries*), and whom I am now presenting as a master psychologist.

How did this transformation occur? Or rather, to put the question in the proper Ursinological terms, How did Winnie-the-Pooh's psychological expertise bring it about? To answer this question we must trace Piglet's progress, pausing at each step to examine how Pooh assists that progress.

## *Piglet's first appearance*

In the most literal sense his first appearance in *Winnie-the-Pooh* is in the Shepard illustration that shows a group of Pooh's friends rescuing Pooh when he had become 'a Wedged Bear in Great Tightness'.

We have previously examined the general problems of this incident, and revealed its true meaning. Now we must concentrate on Piglet's part in it. Shepard shows him tugging at a mouse's tail and himself being tugged by another mouse. The text does not name him at all. We can infer from this that he displayed a praiseworthy desire to help, but that his part was distinctly a minor one.

It is in the next chapter that we see how the author begins to show us in what sense we are to understand his statement in the Introduction that the whole book is about

Piglet. Here also we see Piglet taking the first, rather hesitant steps on the journey that takes him from Christopher Robin's pocket to Pooh's house.

The first paragraph of the new chapter is full of information of the utmost significance about Piglet's psychological situation and the needs resulting from it. We read that

> The Piglet lived in a very grand house in the middle of a beech-tree, and the beech-tree was in the middle of the Forest, and the Piglet lived in the middle of the house.

The picture of Piglet, 'a Very Small Animal', living by himself in a very grand house immediately suggests a certain isolation, while the emphasis on his being in the middle of Forest, of the tree and of the house even more strongly suggests a timid shrinking from the outer world.

As we shall see, this was a part, but only a part, of his character. The shrinking into an inner fortress was counteracted by a love of company. He was also anxious to assert ancestral ties. On the broken sign outside his house is the inscription TRESPASSERS W. He declares that this stood for Trespassers William, and that this was his grandfather's name. A little later, assisting Pooh to track a Woozle, he passes 'the time by telling Pooh what his Grandfather Trespassers W had done to Remove Stiffness after Tracking, and how his Grandfather Trespassers W had suffered in his later years from Shortness of Breath, and other matters of interest . . .'

While no Pooh lover would ever accuse Milne of harsh satire, I fear that some have suspected a gentle mockery when Milne describes Piglet's reminiscences as 'matters of interest'. This, of course, entirely fails to recognize that these were indeed matters of great professional interest to their immediate audience: Winnie-the-Pooh in his capacity of therapist. Only within this frame of reference can we understand why Pooh was 'wondering what a Grandfather was like, and if perhaps this was Two Grandfathers they were after now'. Of all the possible interpretations, the one clearly relevant in this context is that Pooh was considering what Piglet's conception of a grandfather might be. We should, I think, ponder a few of most obvious of the thoughts that might have been passing through his Enormous Brain.

1. Though Piglet held so tenaciously to his interpretation of TRESPASSERS W as his grandfather's name, Trespassers William, was he aware of the more conventional reading, 'Trespassers will be prosecuted'?

2. If he was, was he a proto-Rambler, transforming a threatening exclusion into a familial welcome. Conversely, did he unconsciously fear the unknown ancestor as a menacing intruder?

3. Did the possibility of Two Grandfathers indicate that Piglet might be holding both these concepts? As Pooh knew perfectly well, the unconscious can easily accommodate two contradictory beliefs at the same time.

4. Following this train of thought, Pooh might have made a daring extrapolation from Melanie Klein's concept of the Good Mother and the Bad Mother (see Case 5, p. 125) to a concept of the Good and the Bad Grandfather.

5. Was this double nature represented by the two names 'Woozle' and 'Wizzle'? This may be considered too speculative, yet in the context of tracking, it is hard to avoid it.

6. Wondering whether he would be allowed to take one of the grandfathers home and keep it is a neatly figurative way of hoping he will succeed in relieving Piglet of the burden of his unconscious fear and taking a record of it home for his casebook.

When he wonders what Christopher Robin would say, we can hardly doubt that he is envisaging a dramatic scene when Christopher Robin learns the psychological complexities of the little creature he had so casually taken to school in his pocket.

While even the most superficial reader must have noticed that the picture confirms that 'Piglet was brushing away the snow in front of his house', some may have missed the detail of Piglet's washing hanging on the line behind him. One of the two items is a pair of long johns, the other seems to be something like a tea-cloth or perhaps a table napkin. Thus we see representatives of the personal and of the household washing. Taken in combination with the clearing of the snow, we have a vivid, we might say a symbolic portrayal of a Piglet anxious to present himself as a respectable householder and conscientious housekeeper.

All this reinforces our opinion that he had a strong need for a well established position in society. This also prepares us for his quasi-filial attitude first to Christopher Robin and later to Winnie-the-Pooh.

## Pooh's first treatment of Piglet

We now progress from our preliminary analysis of Piglet's condition to examine the first account of prolonged interaction between Piglet and Pooh. In our present work, we can hardly doubt that this will prove to be the first session in Pooh's treatment of Piglet's psychological problems.

Though Pooh as usual employs an eclectic approach, his treatment of Piglet is dominantly Jungian. This fits in well with his characteristic refusal to dictate to his little friend or even to decide in advance how Piglet's problems would be solved. As Jung himself wrote, 'I knew that such solutions can only come about in an individual way that cannot be foreseen.'

This attitude of relaxed watchfulness informs the beginning of Pooh's treatment of Piglet. We see how subtly Pooh proceeds. Far from making a direct approach to Piglet's problems or even to Piglet himself, Pooh appears to be absorbed in his own concerns. 'Pooh was walking round and round in a circle, thinking of something else, and when Piglet called to him, he just went on walking.'

Thus he arouses Piglet's curiosity, knowing intuitively that his own curious circular movements speak to the maze of Piglet's unconscious. When Piglet asks what he is doing, Pooh's cryptic answers that he is hunting or tracking further stimulate his little friend's curiosity. Four sentences call for our special attention:

> 'Tracking what?' said Piglet, coming closer.
> 'That's just what I ask myself. I ask myself, What?'
> 'What do you think you'll answer?'
> 'I shall have to wait until I catch up with it,' said Winnie-the-Pooh.

The first and third sentences illustrate Pooh's success in arousing Piglet's interest. The second and fourth unmistakably support what we have already said about Pooh's technique in this case. Indeed, when Jung wrote that individual solutions could not be foreseen, he was obviously paraphrasing Pooh's 'I shall have to wait until I catch up with it.'

Even at this early stage in the Piglet case, we may look ahead a little and see that 'it' is the nature of the problem that lies at the root of Piglet's excessive timidity and dependence on others. Pooh must have been pleased when Piglet himself gave an important, indeed a vital, clue by asking, with 'a little squeak of excitement . . . "Oh, Pooh! Do you think it's a – a – a Woozle?"'

Pooh's response, 'It may be – Sometimes it is, and sometimes it isn't. You never can tell with paw-marks', evidences his truly scientific caution in identifying the elusive monsters that lurk in the depths of the unconscious. Again, however, he must have been encouraged by Piglet's reactions. Piglet's excitement indicates his realization that something important is in question, while his strongly marked hesitation before uttering the name 'Woozle' equally indicates fear.

It is all the more to Piglet's credit that, despite this fear and being 'a Very Small Animal', he does not hesitate to join Pooh in the search for the Woozle, even in the face of Pooh's warning that the Woozles – now increased to two – might prove to be Hostile Animals.

This was a turning point in Piglet's progress. Every therapy of the sort Pooh was now employing requires all analysands at some stage to confront their deepest fear. Though obstacles remained and there would be setbacks to be recovered from, Pooh now had solid reasons for being confident that Piglet would persevere to final success.

Meanwhile Pooh and Piglet together go round and round a small larch spinney. Piglet's still undeveloped courage is strained to the utmost when he hears they are now pursuing three Woozles and one Wizzle. Nevertheless, though he starts making excuses to depart, he does not panic but remains with Pooh until they meet Christopher Robin, with whom, Piglet says, Pooh will be safe. Only then do we read that 'he trotted off home as quickly as he could, very glad to be Out of All Danger again'.

Then comes one of those passages which have so often been taken as evidence, and evidence supported out of his own mouth, that Pooh is a Bear of Very Little Brain. By this time, my readers will naturally be inclined to dismiss this as self-evidently absurd. Though this is, of course, the fundamentally correct response, we must always remember that it is our Ursinological duty – and often a personal pleasure as well – to correct error and to dispel ignorance. Let us therefore perform that duty.

After Piglet has gone, Christopher Robin joins Pooh, whom he addresses, with deplorable disrespect as "Silly old Bear", and asks what he was doing in his circumambulations of the spinney. Then Pooh 'sat down and thought, in the most thoughtful way he could think.' Could Milne have made it clearer that we are to expect some thought especially profound, even by the standards of the Enormous Brain from which it emanates?

Alas that such a clear signal should have been so generally ignored! That Pooh's exclamation, 'I have been Foolish and Deluded, and I am a Bear of No Brain at All' should have been grotesquely misinterpreted. That some – though none, I hope, of my present readers – have supposed that Pooh had taken his own and Piglet's repeated footprints as the tracks of a hypothetical Woozle and that only now had he recognized the truth and reproached himself for a truly foolish error.

There may still be some who, fighting a hopeless rearguard action, ask how we explain Pooh's words of undoubted self-reproach in any other way. They, of course, rose from his having lapsed from professional confidentiality by, however inadvertently, letting an uninstructed observer watch and inevitably misunderstand, an example of Pooh's professional treatment. He may also have been saddened by yet another example of the layman's patronising incomprehension of the art of therapy.

I would also call attention to the phrase 'a Bear of No Brain at All'. Even the lesser brains that surround him do not normally say he has *no* brain; only that he has a very little one. Pooh's hyperbolical expression dramatically expresses the frustration that a genius feels at the slightest deviation from the very highest standards.

Thus readers who misunderstand Pooh's words most obviously fail to grasp the central fact of his Enormous Brain. As the last paragraph demonstrates, they also reveal their failure to examine and ponder every word and every implication of the Milnean texts.

Fortunately, the chapter on the Woozle ends on a happier note. Christopher Robin may be blind to the greatness of Pooh, but he is consistently benevolent. Seeing Pooh upset for a moment, he responds admirably:

'You're the Best Bear in All the World', said Christopher Robin soothingly.
'Am I?' said Pooh hopefully. And then he brightened up suddenly.
'Anyhow,' he said, 'it's nearly Luncheon Time.'

I think we can take Pooh's reaction to this somewhat

patronising phrase as indicating a benign acceptance of his friend's goodwill; even perhaps a recognition that moral virtue may be as valuable as intellectual wisdom.

## A major turning point in Piglet's progress

The next stage in Piglet's progress is in Chapter Five of *Winnie-the-Pooh*. This has the significant title 'In which Piglet meets a Heffalump'. In our present context this must mean that here Piglet has to confront his deepest fear, the reality that eluded him in the Woozle.

Working, as Pooh is doing here, in Jungian terms, we recognize that he is concerned with Piglet's shadow and with archetypes or an archetype. Though these are often treated separately, Jung himself wrote, 'The archetypes most clearly characterized from the empirical point of view are the shadow, the anima, and the animus.'

Jung's theory of archetypes is part of his theory of the collective unconscious. As this has been widely misunderstood, a few words of explanation are in order here. Jung argued that we each possessed three layers of mind: (i) a personal conscious, (ii) a personal unconscious, and (iii) a collective unconscious.

There is no problem about accepting a personal conscious. That is the mind we are all aware of. Since Freud, most of us have also met the concept of a personal unconscious, whether or not we accept it. Jung's experience as a therapist convinced him that the unconscious contained material that, unlike the personal unconscious, could not have arisen from personal experience alone. He found this material in a wide variety of people. Even more strikingly, he found evidence of it in cultures separated by vast gaps in time and place, and especially in mythology. This material lived in what he called the collective unconscious, and he described it as having a 'universal, and impersonal nature which is identical in all individuals'.

This concept has been attacked as unacceptably mystical. Jung emphatically rejected this accusation. Everyone, he pointed out, accepts the existence of instincts. Instincts are impersonal and universal and they have a powerful influence on our psyches. He further argued that the analogy between instincts and archetypes is so close 'that there is good reason for supposing that the archetypes are the unconscious images of the instincts themselves'.

Having disposed of any suspicion that Pooh was departing from his normal scientific and rational approach, we now return to his handling the case of Piglet.

The chapter begins with Christopher Robin, Piglet and Pooh picnicking together. Christopher Robin says, 'I saw a Heffalump to-day, Piglet.' He spoke, we are told, 'carelessly', but notice how eagerly Piglet pounces on the subject. 'I saw one once,' said Piglet. 'At least I think I did,' he said. 'Only perhaps it wasn't.'

His confused and half-contradictory words admirably express the state of mind of one who is approaching the dreaded confrontation with the Shadow. Dreaded because 'to become conscious of it involves recognizing the dark aspects of the personality as present and real.' These last words may provoke an indignant protest that we cannot really conceive of a dark side to the harmless and lovable Piglet. This protest is very natural, but it overlooks the fundamental fact that makes Ursinology a legitimate subject of scholarly analysis. It achieves, indeed demands, this kind of study precisely because of its profound depth and universal range.

Obviously in a work ostensibly addressed to children, there is much that it would be inappropriate to bring to the surface. With exquisite tact, Milne preserves the conventions of the genre, while with equal subtlety he gives clues to the more mature reader. Milne's Introduction explicitly tells us that Piglet is 'jealous because he thinks Pooh is having a Grand Introduction all to himself'. On several occasions, he displays marked timidity and clearly suffers from this. True, his sufferings are presented as slight and even comic. Yet they are genuine sufferings, and it is Pooh's task to cure them by the appropriate therapy. In Jungian terms, this necessarily involves bringing Piglet face to face with his Shadow. That this is about to happen now is implied by the contrast between the titles of Chapters Three and Five of *Winnie-the-Pooh*. The former told us that Pooh and Piglet 'nearly catch a Woozle'. Now we read 'Piglet meets a Heffalump'.

After Piglet's tentative claim that he has seen a Heffalump, '"So did I," said Pooh, wondering what a Heffalump was like.' This means, of course, that he was considering the precise form that Piglet's Shadow would take. His thoughts lead him to a firm decision. After walking homewards together for some time, Pooh announced:

> 'Piglet, I have decided something.'
> 'What have you decided, Pooh?'
> 'I have decided to catch a Heffalump.'

The moment has come for the vital confrontation. Pooh understands that a direct intellectual approach would be useless; a judgement amply confirmed by Piglet's literal interpretation of all Pooh says. He has concluded that Piglet has now reached the stage when he is ready for the ordeal of meeting his Shadow. So Pooh sets up a psychodrama: a deliberately staged event that will bring him face to face with this awe-inspiring figure.

Piglet digs a pit as a Heffalump trap, which Pooh himself baits with honey. Having carried out this absurd

plan for catching a Heffalump, they both go to bed, agreeing to meet at six o'clock next morning and see how many Heffalumps they have caught in their trap.

Both have bad nights. Piglet is troubled by nightmarish visions of his archetypal Shadow: nightmares which we can understand though he cannot. Pooh, confident his plan will have the desired therapeutic effect, is untroubled in mind. He does, however, wake up hungry. A reminder that even the greatest psychologists are not immune from commonplace bodily desires.

He goes to find the pot of honey he had placed in the Heffalump trap. Prudently anxious not to waste any of it, Pooh pushes his head so far into the jar that he gets stuck there. There it is when Piglet, torn between fear and curiosity, creeps to the edge of the Heffalump Trap and looks down. In this situation, Freud would have feared for his dignity and authority. Most therapists would have been nonplussed. Pooh remained master of the situation. He saw at once that his apparently humiliating position offered a golden opportunity to fulfil his plan for confronting Piglet with his Shadow.

> So at last he lifted up his head, jar and all, and made a loud, roaring noise of Sadness and Despair . . . and it was at that moment that Piglet looked down.
>
> 'Help, help!' cried Piglet, 'a Heffalump, a Horrible Heffalump!' and he scampered off as hard as he could, still crying out, 'Help, help, a Herrible Hoffalump! Hoff, Hoff, a Hellible Horralump! Holl, Holl, a

Hoffable Hellarump!' And he didn't stop crying and scampering until he got to Christopher Robin's house.

Even in the safety of Christopher Robin's house, he still struggles for words to describe what he has seen. He does finally utter a striking phrase: 'A huge big . . . like an enormous big nothing.' This phrase, direct from Piglet's immediate experience, unsophisticated by later elaboration, was doubtless in Jung's mind when he wrote 'The term "archetype" designates only those psychic contents which have not yet been submitted to conscious elaboration and are therefore an immediate datum of psychic experience.'

Emboldened by Christopher Robin's company, Piglet returns to the Heffalump Trap and discovers the truth. His first reaction is painful. 'Then Piglet saw what a Foolish Piglet he had been, and he was so ashamed of himself that he ran straight off home and went to bed with a headache.' Piglet's reaction is entirely normal in the circumstances. Confronting one's Shadow is always deeply painful. It is also deeply embarrassing. For it forces one to recognize those parts of one's character that one finds repulsive and shameful. The Heffalump that Piglet confronted was a ferocious monster, the exact opposite of the timid Piglet. He had to realize this fierce creature was hidden deep within himself. This experience leaves one in a state of shock and ready to take to one's bed.

Our first reaction might also be uncomfortable. Was this an example of successful therapy — poor Piglet first terrified, then embarrassed and suffering a headache? Second thoughts, however, must surely convince us that one brief shock and a temporary embarrassment were a price worth paying for a permanent cure. No wonder Pooh went off to breakfast with Christopher Robin well content with himself.

The fact that he goes off with Christopher Robin has interesting implications. Can we doubt that here was another example of Pooh's technique of enlisting the help of others in his therapy? He must have foreseen that the panic-stricken Piglet would seek refuge in Christopher Robin's house and that, 'emboldened by Christopher Robin's company', he would return to the Heffalump Trap. Now that Piglet had seen that this 'enormous big nothing', was simply Winnie-the-Pooh with his head stuck in a honey jar, he truly understands the folly of his fears at the deepest possible level. Though he still has some way to go before he can become positively brave, his fears in future will be rational and therefore manageable.

While Pooh follows a mainly Jungian approach to Piglet's problems, we should be surprised if we did not find examples of his characteristic eclecticism. And of course we do. Piglet's terrified reaction to the Heffalump, and especially his likening it to 'an enormous big nothing', inescapably turn our minds to the Gestalt therapy of Frederick Perls (1893–1970). Perls describes a frightening nothingness and helplessness as the 'impasse' that we have to confront and pass through if we are to mature.

Whatever psychological theory we favour, we are bound to recognize a turning point in Piglet's progress, a progress that fully justifies Pooh's therapy.

*Piglet progresses further*

So much for a narrative of events. What now about the explanation? What was the deep inner fear embodied in the monstrous vision of the Horrible Heffalump? If we put Piglet's early timidity side by side with its symbols – his dwelling surrounded by concentric protective walls and his recourse to Christopher Robin's pocket when venturing into the outer world – the answer is plain. He had been suffering a paranoid fear of the outer world. His unconscious had felt it as a jungle of terrifying monsters, all the more terrifying for being indefinable and shapeless. This in turn rose from his profound unconscious fear of the repressed fierce side hidden within himself.

Pooh is obviously and justifiably pleased with Piglet's progress when they next meet. This occurs when Pooh has hurried home to get a present for Eeyore, whom he has found exceptionally depressed because nobody has remembered his birthday.

Pooh finds Piglet jumping up and down, trying to reach the knocker of Pooh's front door. Pooh knocks for him and comments,

> 'What a long time whoever lives here is answering this door.' And he knocked again
>> 'But Pooh,' said Piglet, 'it's your own house!'
>> 'Oh!,' said Pooh. 'So it is,' he said. 'Well, let's go in.'

Even the most sceptical can hardly doubt that Pooh is

merely pretending he does not recognize his own door in order to test Piglet's reaction. He has now gained sufficient confidence in his own judgement to point out Pooh's apparent error. Pooh confirms this by agreeing ('So it is') and inviting Piglet in – an obvious preview of his later invitation to join Pooh permanently.

He commends Piglet's suggestion of a balloon as a suitable present for Eeyore. While Pooh goes off to ask Owl to write a birthday inscription on the honey jar, Piglet runs off, carrying his balloon for Eeyore. But a rabbit hole causes him to fall flat on his face. What follows deserves minute analysis as evidence of his now strengthened psyche.

BANG!!!???***!!!

Piglet lay there, wondering what had happened. At first he thought that the whole world had blown up; and then he thought that perhaps only the Forest part of it had; and then he thought that perhaps only *he* had; and he was now alone in the moon or somewhere, and would never see Christopher Robin or Pooh or Eeyore again. And then he thought, 'Well, even if I'm in the moon, I needn't be face downwards all the time,' so he got cautiously up and looked about him.

Here we follow step by step the thoughts that chase across Piglet's mind after the explosion. It is more than doubtful if the untreated Piglet could have sustained the physical shock followed by such a succession of terrifying ideas: the apocalyptic concept of the end of the world; the concept of total aloneness in the moon or somewhere not even identifiable; the permanent loss of his friends. Even the steadiest nerves might give way in such a dire situation. Yet, far from losing his nerve, Piglet calmly tells himself that wherever he may be, there is no need to stay in the uncomfortable prone position.

In fact, Piglet now enjoys some of the benefits of having faced his Shadow. He has assimilated some of the boldness he had previously rejected

Having got up and realized the true situation, he is naturally somewhat downcast to find his balloon reduced to a 'small piece of damp rag'. Saddened but undeterred, he carries out his mission. He is still far from happy when Pooh arrives carrying the Useful Pot, but cheers up when he sees Eeyore's pleasure in repeatedly putting the burst balloon into the Useful Pot.

'So it does!' said Pooh. 'It goes in!'

'So it does!' said Piglet. 'And it comes out!'

'Doesn't it?' said Eeyore. 'It goes in and out like anything.

'I'm very glad," said Pooh happily, 'that I thought of giving you a Useful Pot to put things in.'

'I'm very glad,' said Piglet happily, 'that I thought of giving you Something to put in a Useful Pot.'

By the end of this chapter, then, we see that Piglet had not only passed a most severe test but had been rewarded by the approbation of Pooh and the happiness of Eeyore. A triumph for Piglet, and also of course a triumph for Pooh as his therapist. E. H. Shepard's tailpiece to the chapter sums up the situation perfectly: Pooh and Piglet walk off together, happily hand in hand, while Eeyore is equally happy in taking the remains of the balloon in and out of the Useful Pot.

## *Piglet's new found courage is put to the test again in the next episode*

Rabbit's plan for driving Kanga and Roo out of the Forest cast Piglet in the daunting role of replacing Roo in Kanga's pouch, while Rabbit carried the real Roo away. With a perfectly rational caution, Piglet asks whether it is wise to provoke the wrath of one of the Fiercer Animals when doubly fierce because deprived of its young.

Rabbit's rather contemptuous 'Piglet, you haven't any pluck' receives an answer highly significant of Piglet's state of mind at this stage: 'It is hard to be brave,' said Piglet, sniffing slightly, 'when you're only a Very Small Animal.' He feels an understandable alarm but it is no longer the blind panic that rose from his unconscious with overwhelming power. On the contrary, while admitting it is *hard* for him to be brave, he does not shirk the challenge. When Rabbit explains his importance in the plan, 'Piglet was so excited at the idea of being Useful that he forgot to be frightened any more.'

Jean-Paul Sartre (1905–1980), perhaps a better psychologist than a philosopher, might well have been thinking of Piglet when he wrote, 'what produces cowardice is the act of giving up or giving way; and a temperament is not an action . . . the coward makes himself cowardly, the hero makes himself heroic.'

When the time comes to test Piglet's resolution in action, he does not flinch. At the right moment, he jumps into Kanga's pouch, and remembers to make 'a squeaky Roo-noise from the bottom of Kanga's pocket' when she asks if Roo is all right. He does not enjoy the journey in Kanga's pouch as she returns home in a series of large jumps. He keeps his nerve after his Terrifying Journey, and says 'Aha!' It is not a very convincing 'Aha!' but we cannot blame Piglet for this. Kanga has realized the situation and is playing her own little joke, which involves pretending to mistake Piglet for Roo.

Roo's nightly routine includes having a bath. This alone would have been repugnant to Piglet, but when Kanga suggests the additional horror of a *cold* bath, he said 'in as brave a voice as he could: "Kanga, I see the time has come to spleak painly." ' He continues to protest unavailingly until he seizes the chance to escape through the door that Christopher Robin has left open. Immediately before his escape, he had suffered yet another traumatic experience. When Christopher Robin arrives, Piglet confidently appeals to him to confirm his true identity.

> 'There you are!' said Piglet. 'I told you so. I'm Piglet.'
> Christopher Robin shook his head again.
> 'Oh, you're not Piglet,' he said. 'I know Piglet well, and he's *quite* a different colour.'

Few things are more deeply disturbing than to have one's own identity denied, and to be given a new one: 'Henry Pootel'. The shock to Piglet was all the worse because it came from Christopher Robin, whom he had always regarded as a uniquely reliable and benevolent protector.

The powerful effect of Pooh's therapy is impressively demonstrated by Piglet's resilience after this series of shocks. He quickly restores himself 'to his own nice comfortable colour again' by rolling on the ground. With a generosity of spirit that can come only from a mind at peace with itself, he forgave Christopher Robin for his share in the trials of that day. For we read that 'every Tuesday Piglet spent the day with his great friend Christopher Robin'.

It is still a little surprising perhaps that Piglet's faith in Christopher Robin remains unshaken. When Pooh tells him about the Expotition to the North Pole, Piglet is worried at the thought they might find something fierce with teeth – 'But if Christopher Robin is coming I don't mind anything.' We can infer from Pooh's silence that he is content with Piglet's state of mind. Piglet would never have a positively adventurous nature. Nevertheless, his response to the projected Expotition can hardly be faulted. He makes prudent enquiries into the risks involved; decides there is adequate protection, and joins. There is no question of his suddenly remembering he had to do something that had to be done on a fine day when everyone else was on an Expotition.

Though he plays a minor part in this episode, he does make one remark that shows a notable growth in confidence. When Christopher Robin warns his followers that they are coming to ' just the place for an ambush', Pooh whispers to Piglet, 'What sort of bush? A gorse-bush?'

'My dear Pooh,' said Owl in his superior way, 'don't you know what an Ambush is?'

'Owl,' said Piglet, looking round at him severely,

'Pooh's whisper was a perfectly private whisper, and there was no need —'

Pooh must have been secretly delighted by Piglet's boldness.

## *Piglet keeps his nerve when virtually marooned*

The title of Milne's next chapter proclaims that Piglet is at its very centre, both literally and figuratively: 'In which Piglet is entirely surrounded by water'. As the rain continues to pour down, Piglet's first regret is that he is alone and unable to share the excitement of the flood with any of his friends. As the water rises, 'It's a little Anxious,' he said to himself, 'to be a Very Small Animal Entirely Surrounded by Water.'

Though anxious, he never comes near to panic. He calmly considers, one by one, how his friends might cope with the situation. He imagines a possible and appropriate solution for each of them, but feels 'I can't do *anything.*'

Then he remembers Christopher Robin's story of a man on a desert island who had put a message in a bottle and thrown the bottle into the sea. So Piglet followed his example, appealing on one side of the paper, for

HELP!
PIGLIT (ME)

and on the other:

IT'S ME PIGLIT, HELP HELP!

He now faces the situation with admirable calm and realism. He has done all he can do to save himself:

> 'So now,' he thought, 'somebody else will have to do something, and I hope they will do it soon, because if they don't I shall have to swim, which I can't, so I hope they do it soon.' And he gave a very long sigh and said, 'I wish Pooh were here. It's so much more friendly with two.'

Again, no hint of panic. Significantly, it is now Pooh whose company he specially desires. And we all know how Pooh played the leading part in Piglet's physical rescue, as he was already doing in his psychological rescue. It is perhaps typical of uninformed opinion that Pooh's rescue of Piglet from the flood was celebrated by a feast in his honour, while the psychological benefits he bestowed on all his friends went uncelebrated, because unnoticed.

## Piglet as Pooh's active assistant

Piglet's growing maturity and consequently the development of his friendship with Winnie-the-Pooh are both emphasised at the beginning of *The House at Pooh Corner*. The very first sentence tells us that Pooh Bear 'went round to Piglet's house to see what Piglet was doing'. Finding Piglet not at home, Pooh returns to his own home, to find 'Piglet sitting in his best arm-chair'. Pooh seems perfectly happy that Piglet has made himself so completely at home, and invites him to join in a 'little smackerel of something'.

On the other hand, Pooh is not going to let Piglet become the 1920s equivalent of a couch potato. Although it is snowing heavily, the two of them are soon on their way to Eeyore to sing him a new song Pooh has composed. As the snow goes on falling, 'in a little while Piglet was wearing a white muffler round his neck and feeling more snowy behind the ears than he had ever felt before'. He does not enjoy this, but with his newfound strength of mind 'he didn't want Pooh to think he was Giving In'. So he merely suggests they should practise the song at home and sing it to Eeyore at some future date.

His still somewhat wavering resolution is reinforced by Pooh's physical presence and example. Here we have one of the many allusions to learning by modelling; in this case to Piglet's learning to soldier on through the snow, modelling his behaviour on Pooh's. Work on this area is especially associated with Albert Bandura's 'behaviour modification'.

Piglet follows Pooh in joining in Pooh's Outdoor Song which Has To Be Sung In The Snow. He does, though, show independent judgement when he comments on the song's emphasis on cold toes: 'Pooh,' he said solemnly, 'it isn't the *toes* so much as the *ears*.'

When they have warmed themselves up by singing Pooh's song six times, Pooh speaks movingly of poor Eeyore's houseless condition and says, 'Let's build him a house.' Piglet hails this as 'a Grand Idea'. The story of Eeyore's house belongs to the chapter on Eeyore. All we need specially notice here is Piglet's vigorously *active* benevolence, a benevolence realized in co-operation with Pooh. A minor symptom of his greater ease with himself is his cautious self-congratulation on his part in contributing the 'tiddely-poms' to Pooh's song. 'And I know it *seems* easy,' said Piglet to himself, 'but it isn't *every one* who could do it.'

## Piglet controls his uneasiness with Tigger

When introduced to Tigger, Piglet is generous in his offer of haycorns but cautiously puts the table between him and his bouncy guest. Wisely, too, 'he got close to Pooh and felt much braver'. Intuitively he felt Pooh as a source of strength. Once more we notice that, despite some qualms, he remains calm. Indeed, he behaves with considerable social aplomb. When he discovers that Tiggers don't like haycorns, but that thistles are what they like best: 'Then let's go along and see Eeyore,' said Piglet. When Eeyore is introduced to Tigger and almost immediately asks, 'When is he going?' Piglet smoothes a potentially awkward situation by explaining to Tigger 'that he mustn't mind what Eeyore said because he was *always* gloomy'.

Piglet's critical powers ripen with his growing confidence. Tigger's rejection of honey, haycorns and thistles inspires a new poem by Pooh, beginning:

> What shall we do about poor little Tigger?
> If he never eats nothing he'll never get bigger.
>
> 'He's quite big enough anyhow,' said Piglet.
> 'He isn't *really* very big.'
> 'Well, he *seems* so.'

By now, Piglet dares to differ from Pooh, and also makes a subtle distinction between appearance and reality. It is not surprising that 'Pooh was thoughtful when he heard this'. He must have been delighted at this further evidence that his unobtrusive therapy was proving so effective. He pays Piglet the unprecedented compliment of adding a couplet incorporating Piglet's criticism:

> But whatever his weight in pounds, shillings, and ounces,
> He always seems bigger because of his bounces.

Again Piglet displays critical independence, saying he likes the poem except for the shillings: 'I don't think they ought to be there.'

> 'They wanted to come in after the pounds,' explained Pooh, 'so I let them. It is the best way to write poetry, letting things come.'
> 'Oh, I didn't know,' said Piglet.

It is not surprising that Piglet did not know, but we can make an educated guess that Pooh was trying a Surrealist mode of poetry, one which its theorists linked especially with the unconscious, and therefore with the juxtaposition of strikingly dissimilar objects.

## Piglet's triumph

Having followed the progress of Pooh's treatment of Piglet in detail until we have seen repeated evidence of its success, we may now pass on rapidly to the final apotheosis of the 'Very Small Animal'. Piglet's delight at the remembered blueness of Christopher Robin's braces reassures us that inner calm has not deprived him of perceptual vividness. Nor has it deprived him of compassion and generosity, as we see when he brings a bunch of violets to Eeyore. When lost in the mist while unbouncing Tigger, Piglet shows no more than a proper confidence in Pooh. In our present context, we are bound to see Pooh's guiding Piglet through the mist to his proper place as a symbol of his therapeutic success.

We now come to the two great climactic moments in Piglet's life. The first occurs when he and Pooh visit Wol and are trapped with him when the gale blew down Wol's tree house, and left a branch blocking his front door. They think of possible ways of escape. Piglet displays both realism and his new found independence when he firmly rejects Pooh's first suggestion that Owl should fly up to the letter-box with Piglet on his back. But he does not lapse into despair as he might so easily have done in the past. When Owl says that it is no good thinking about that plan, Piglet replies, '"Then we'd better think of something else," and began to do so at once'.

It is, as we should expect, the Enormous Brain of Pooh that produces the practical solution. This, as I am sure most of you will recall, is to tie a piece of string to Piglet; then for Owl to fly up to the letter-box, thread the string through the wire and bring the other end to the floor. Pooh and Owl would then pull on the string, thus lifting Piglet to the letter-box, though which he could crawl and summon aid.

Piglet courageously accepts his mission. Pooh's psychological training allows him to see that Piglet is naturally worried by the fear that the string may break. He reassures Piglet about physical safety both by reminding him that a Small Animal will not break the string, and by promising to stand under him. Psychologically he encourages him by suggesting he may win fame in a Respectful Pooh Song. As we all know, the combination of

Pooh's intellect and Piglet's devoted courage proves irresistible. All are saved, and Pooh celebrates Piglet's triumph in a Hum of unprecedented length and metrical complexity.

Piglet is naturally delighted but, with perhaps overscrupulous honesty, protests that, contrary to a passage in the Hum, he did blinch a little. 'Just at first.'

Pooh makes the immortal answer: 'You only blinched inside, and that's the bravest way for a Very Small Animal to blinch that there is.'

> Piglet sighed with happiness, and began to think about himself. He was B R A V E . . .

This brief sentence tells us that Pooh's treatment has achieved the ultimate therapeutic triumph: it has helped Piglet to throw away that lack of self-esteem that had lain at the root of his old timidity and dependence.

A new problem however remains unsolved. Wol and his friends have escaped unharmed, but Wol's house is in ruins. Rabbit, now using his organizational skills to excellent advantage, announces:

I AM SCERCHING FOR A NEW HOUSE
FOR OWL SO HAD YOU RABBIT

It is rather surprising that the first to answer this appeal should be Eeyore. This reminds us of the enormous advance he had made in social awareness and active benevolence. However, when he reveals the house he has found for Wol, it is, in fact, Piglet's house. Eeyore's long isolation in his damp part of the Forest accounts for his failure to recognize Piglet's house; a failure all the more understandable, because, like Owl's old house, it is in a tree.

However innocently, Eeyore has created an embarrassing situation. Nobody wants to discourage his awkward early steps in active benevolence. Equally, nobody wants to dispossess Piglet. It is Piglet himself who has to answer the first question. 'Just the house for Owl. Don't you think so, little Piglet?'

Inspired by Pooh's hum, 'then Piglet did a Noble Thing'.

> 'Yes, it's just the house for Owl,' he said grandly. 'And I hope he'll be very happy in it.' And then he gulped twice, because he had been very happy in it himself.

Despite Piglet's noble gesture, there is uneasiness. Even

Eeyore feels this and he appeals to Christopher Robin. In the course of the Pooh saga, Christopher Robin has shown increasing negotiating skill. Now he utters a tactfully worded question:

> 'Well,' he said at last, 'it's a very nice house, and if your own house is blown down, you *must* go somewhere else, mustn't you, Piglet? What would you do, if *your* house was blown down?'
>
> Before Piglet could think, Pooh answered for him.
>
> 'He'd come and live with me,' said Pooh, 'Wouldn't you, Piglet?'
>
> Piglet squeezed his paw. 'Thank you, Pooh,' he said, 'I should love to.'

And so ends Piglet's progress from Christopher Robin's pocket to Winnie-the-Pooh's house.

## Case 3

### Pooh at his most eclectic with Tigger

Tigger was the most multi-faceted character that Pooh had to deal with, and he presented a special psychological challenge. His natural ebullience was at first too much for Rabbit, who called it 'bounciness' and made an unsuccessful plan to eradicate it, as we shall see in Case 4.

Piglet shared Rabbit's attitude and so did Eeyore. On the other hand, Kanga welcomed him immediately, recognized his need for affection and made him thoroughly at home. Most strikingly, she entrusted her beloved Roo to his care.

### Pooh hears a strange noise in the night

In these circumstances, our obvious course is to begin with a detailed analysis of Tigger's first appearance. Most significantly, it is to Winnie-the-Pooh himself. A strange noise wakens Pooh in the middle of the night. He establishes that the noise was not made by anybody trying to get into his honey-cupboard, nor by Piglet, Christopher Robin or Eeyore. He tries to get back to sleep, 'But the noise went on.'

'Worraworraworraworraworra,' said Whatever-it-was, and Pooh found he wasn't asleep after all.

'What can it be?' he thought.

He mentally reviews the usual Forest noises – growl, purr, bark – and 'the noise you make before beginning a piece of poetry'. He firmly dismisses them and concludes 'it's a noise of some kind, made by a strange animal! And he's making it outside my door. So I shall get up and ask him not to do it.'

Even at this preliminary stage, there is much for us to notice. First we observe the scientific, systematic way in which Pooh reviews the evidence and comes to a logical conclusion. Next we notice that his conclusion is not exclusively intellectual but one that leads him to action. Thus he combines the abstract approach of psychology's parent, philosophy, with the practical approach of psychology proper.

It is also clear that Pooh's own psyche is in the healthiest condition. Many of us, if wakened by a strange noise in the middle of the night, would feel a certain nervousness. The weaker among us might try to fool ourselves into believing we had made a mistake in dismissing the commonplace Forest noises. The braver would investigate, but either apprehensively or with a somewhat artificial aggressiveness. Pooh, free from all such weaknesses, shows a cool curiosity.

He got out of bed and opened his front door.

'Hallo!' said Pooh, in case there was anything outside.

'Hallo!' said Whatever-it-was.

'Oh!' said Pooh. 'Hallo!'

'Hallo!'

'Oh, *there* you are!' said Pooh. 'Hallo!'

'Hallo!' said the Strange Animal, wondering how long this was going on.

Pooh was just going to say 'Hallo!' for the fourth time when he thought that he wouldn't, so he said 'Who is it?' instead.

Seldom has the text pointed us so clearly towards a particular psychological theory. Three 'Hallos' and almost a fourth from Pooh, and three from the unknown visitor. Indeed we might think the emphasis was somewhat laboured were it not for the fact that no previous commentator has picked up the obvious reference to Eric Berne's *What Do You Say After You Say Hello?* (1972)

In this instance, what Pooh says after both parties have said 'Hallo', several times, is 'Who is it?' After Tigger has identified himself, Pooh invites him to spend the night in his, Pooh's, house and join him for breakfast in the morning.

Again we are impressed with Pooh's calm fearlessness when confronted with a totally strange kind of animal. If we were misguided enough to question Pooh's judgement, we might doubt his wisdom in inviting this strange unknown into his house. Surely we might think that rejection of xenophobia can fall into rash trust in unknown persons. As we should expect, the results fully justify Pooh's decision. Once more, we notice how wrong it is ever to doubt the Wisdom of Pooh.

## Stroking Tigger

References to Eric Berne continue. Berne was the founder of Transactional Analysis (TA). A transaction in Berne's sense occurs whenever two people meet and one acknowledges the other's presence, either by speaking or in some other way. Berne calls this a transactional stimulus. The other's reaction is a transactional response.

Berne believes that we all have what he calls 'stimulus-hunger'. If we are deprived of this, our psychic health will be seriously, even fatally, damaged. Infants need to have this satisfied by physical stroking or similar contact, chiefly with parents. In adult life, such physical contacts are limited to intimates. With others, this need is usually satisfied by symbolic 'stroking'. In this extended sense, 'stroking' includes any recognition of another person's presence. An exchange of these strokes is, in Berne's terminology, a 'transaction'.

Our text does not explicitly state why Tigger came and made a strange noise outside Pooh's house in the middle of the night. But his most obvious motive is to find company; in other words, he was suffering from what Berne calls 'recognition-hunger'. Some readers may wonder why it was to Pooh's house that he came. It is intuitively implausible that it was by mere chance. We need not, however, rely on intuition. As always, Milne has given a clue to the alert reader.

> I'm Tigger,' said Tigger.
> 'Oh!' said Pooh, for he had never seen an animal like this before. 'Does Christopher Robin know about you?'
> 'Of course he does,' said Tigger.

As always, we must pay careful attention to the exact words we are studying. 'Does Christopher Robin know *about* you?' (my emphasis). Pooh is not asking whether Christopher Robin has merely met this strange newcomer but whether he knows about him. That is, whether he knows Tigger's character traits, personality, and, above all his psychological needs.

Now all is clear. We can see just why Tigger came to Pooh's house. Christopher Robin — with more perceptiveness than we have sometimes given him credit for — had seen that Tigger needed the help of the Forest's master psychologist and had directed him to Winnie-the-Pooh. Of course, clients do not normally arrive at a psychologist's house without an appointment, in the middle of the night. Nor do they announce themselves by shouting 'Worraworraworraworraworra'. But this unorthodox approach impresses us with the urgency of Tigger's need and also with his ignorance of what Wol, in a different context, called 'the customary procedure'. We shall return to the latter point later, when we come to see Pooh teaching Social Skills to Tigger.

Meanwhile, Pooh rises to the occasion with his usual blend of professional expertise, personal kindliness and calm commonsense. His expertise enables him to recognize the situation. Let us remember he had gone to the door with the declared intention of asking Whatever-it-was to stop making the noise. Why does he do nothing of the sort? Clearly because he sees that this is an occasion for help, not for even the mildest hint of rebuke. Instead, he applies the appropriate form of 'stroking'.

Pooh's response to the situation is a particularly satisfying example of his judicious eclecticism. Lacan would have made an immediate diagnosis. Berne would have seen a need for stroking. Pooh combines Lacanian swiftness with Bernian recognition of need. And, of course, those familiar with the positive, non-judgemental approach of Carl Rogers will recognize yet another approach. As Rogers was born in 1902, he might well have been directly influenced by the Wisdom of Pooh. However that may be, the 'client-centered therapy' associated with Rogers was highly characteristic of Winnie-the-Pooh.

His natural kindliness reinforces his professional therapeutic approach when he invites Tigger to stay the night and share tomorrow's breakfast with him. He then tells Tigger that 'it's the middle of the night, which is a good time for going to sleep'. This sounds like a commonplace remark, but, as I am sure most readers now realize, it is more. It reminds Tigger that he is part of the real world, which contains much more than his psychological difficulties. This soupçon of cognitive therapy continues in Pooh's reminder that the middle of the night is a good time for going to sleep. Sleep is not only specially needed by the hyperactive Tigger, but is one of those natural rhythms to which he should return after his apparently sleepless night.

Though Pooh is generous and benevolent, he is quite free from any morbid tendency to self-martyrdom. He demonstrates this, when, having ascertained that Tiggers like everything, he concludes that Tigger will like sleeping on the floor, while he goes back to bed. When he adds, 'we'll do things in the morning', he is clearly postponing the next therapeutic session until a more appropriate time.

## Pooh and Lacan

Pooh made snap judgements when he decided that Tigger was (a) harmless and (b) in need of therapy. Both judgements did, of course, turn out to be correct. It must be significant that their first meeting occurs on the opposite page to Shepard's illustration of Tigger looking at his own reflection in Pooh's looking-glass. Can we doubt that this combination should remind us once again of Jacques Lacan (1901–1981). Lacan was famous for his immediate diagnoses and for his emphasis on the mirror image as constituting children's first realizing themselves as

separate beings. Tigger's reaction is unusual: instead of realising himself as separate, he is led to the thought that he is not unique. By providing the environment necessary for Tigger to learn what a looking-glass is, Pooh assists Tigger's adjustment to reality and both anticipates and goes beyond Lacan.

Before continuing with Tigger's progress, let us glance at another Shepard illustration: one that shows Pooh brushing his hair in front of his looking-glass. With Lacan in mind, we may suspect a reference to Lacan's habit of going to a professional beautician for grooming before giving his celebrated seminars.

Now we return to Tigger and the looking-glass. Pooh begins to explain what a looking-glass is but is interrupted by Tigger's fight with the tablecloth. Tigger is reassuringly cheerful when he gets his head out of the tablecloth and asks, 'Have I won?' Nevertheless, there is a touch of paranoia in his assumption that the tablecloth had tried to bite him when he was not looking.

Again Pooh applies cognitive therapy, not only by telling Tigger what a tablecloth is, but by putting the cloth on the table and laying it for breakfast, with a large honey-pot on the cloth.

Even at this early stage, we have seen Pooh treat Tigger with a truly eclectic mixture of therapies: Lacanian in his instant diagnosis and perhaps in a calculated exposure of Tigger to his mirror image; Transactional in his 'stroking'; Cognitive in correcting Tigger's cognitive errors by repeatedly reminding him of the facts. During the morning, the treatment continues.

Cognitively, Tigger's wild statement that Tiggers like everything is corrected by a series of exposures to the relevant facts, which teach Tigger that Tiggers do not like honey, haycorns and thistles. When Tigger does discover that Extract of Malt is what Tiggers like, his delight is in line with Festinger's theory of cognitive consistency and Heider's of cognitive balance. According to these theories, we feel uncomfortable when our beliefs are inconsistent with one another or with perceived facts.

In a narrative ostensibly designed to amuse children, what could be a more vivid example of these theories than seeing Pooh conduct Tigger through a series of experiments with food?

Pooh's eclecticism is especially marked in his treatment of Tigger. This is obviously because he sees that Tigger's case is especially complex and requires an equally complex therapeutic approach. So we are not surprised to find Pooh applying yet more psychological theories, while continuing with some we have already met.

## Kanga and Tigger

After Tigger has discovered that he does not like thistles, Pooh says, 'Come along and we'll go and see Kanga. She's sure to have lots of breakfast for you.'

Tigger goes rushing off with his usual impulsiveness, while Pooh and Piglet follow slowly in silence. Pooh says nothing because he is thinking of a poem, which we now reexamine:

> What shall we do about poor little Tigger?
> If he never eats nothing he'll never get bigger.
> He doesn't like honey and haycorns and thistles

Because of the taste and because of the bristles.
And all the good things which an animal likes
Have the wrong sort of swallow or too many spikes.'

What especially strikes Piglet in these lines is the warning that 'If he never eats nothing he'll never get bigger.'

'He's quite big enough anyhow,' said Piglet.
   'He isn't really very big.'
   'Well, he seems so.'
   Pooh was thoughtful when he heard this, and then he murmured to himself:
   But whatever his weight in pounds, shillings, and
      ounces,
   He always seems bigger because of his bounces.

Let us try to see the connection between Pooh's thoughtfulness, the last lines of his poem, and Tigger. These point to a contrast between objective, measurable fact and subjective impression.

Of course, some part of the subjective impressions are due to the difference between Piglet – a Very Small Animal – and Pooh – a comparatively big one. More importantly perhaps, Pooh first meets Tigger when Tigger is sitting, apparently still. Piglet meets him moving. Pooh had warned Tigger not to be too Bouncy at first when he met Piglet, and Tigger had replied 'that Tiggers were only bouncy before breakfast, and that as soon as they had had a few haycorns they became Quiet and Refined'. But as

Tigger necessarily meets Piglet before breakfast he has not yet reached a Quiet and Refined state. Piglet's reactions seem to support this interpretation. He says, as 'he edged round to the other side of the table, "I thought Tiggers were smaller than that." '

Taking all this together, we must, I think, conclude that we are looking an example of the 'primacy effect' of the eminent American psychologist, Solomon Asch. Asch argued that the first information we get about anything establishes 'a direction which then exerts a continuous effect on the latter terms'. Thus Piglet's exaggerated impression of Tigger's size is at least partly due to his first impression of the bouncy visitor.

On their way to Kanga's house, they meet Christopher Robin, and hug him. Though there was a warm and friendly relation between Pooh and Christopher Robin, this is the only recorded instance of Pooh's hugging him. Why *now*? Clearly Pooh is rewarding his often obtuse friend for the wisdom he had shown in directing Tigger to Pooh.

## Kanga strokes Tigger

When Pooh has brought Tigger to Kanga, we find the flood of psychologically relevant information almost overwhelming. On the level of Transactional Analysis, we see Kanga employing an extremely effective form of 'stroking'. While all recognition of another person's presence is 'stroking' in some sense, we naturally prefer a friendly form of recognition. This Kanga gives in abundance. As soon as she knows that Tigger wants breakfast, 'Kanga said very kindly, "Well, look in my cupboard, Tigger dear, and see what you'd like."'

That is, she not only gives him the material sustenance he needs, but speaks 'very kindly' to him and addresses him as 'dear'. Authorial comment emphasizes that this is more than mere courtesy or even generosity. She acts as she does because she has an immediate intuitive insight into Tigger's emotional as well as his physical needs: 'she knew at once that, however big Tigger seemed to be, he wanted as much kindness as Roo'.

It is also noteworthy that Kanga leaves Tigger free to choose his own food from her larder. This in marked contrast with her firm control of Roo's diet. It points, in terms appropriate to the context, to another important core element in Transactional Analysis. This concerns Eric Berne's analysis of human ego states.

According to this, we all have a limited number of ego states: (i) those which resemble parental figures; (ii) those which are independent and appraise reality; (iii) those which were fixated in early childhood but still remain active. In the technical jargon, these are named respectively: exteropsychic, neopsychic, and archaeopsychic ego states. Dr Berne himself gives permission to use their colloquial equivalents – Parent, Adult, Child – 'in all but the most formal discussions'. I hope my readers will be happy to accept his permission.

Now we see Kanga inviting Tigger to look for and choose his own food, while insisting that Roo shall take his Strengthening Extract of Malt. In the first case, Kanga's

Adult ego state speaks to Tigger's Adult state. In the second, her Parent ego state speaks to Roo's Child ego state. In each case, she uses the state appropriate to the relationship. Berne calls such satisfactory transactions *complementary*. In other places, we shall examine some cases of what Berne calls *crossed transactions*.

What about Pooh in all this? The text tells us that he 'was beginning to feel a little eleven o'clockish. And he found a small tin of condensed milk, and something seemed to tell him that Tiggers didn't like this, so he took it into a corner by itself, and went with it to see that nobody interrupted it.'

I hope it is by now unnecessary to assure my readers that this is no evidence of greed, still less of selfishness, on Pooh's part. But, as long-held prejudices take a lot of uprooting, I feel I must not just assert that Pooh is displaying profound practical professional skill. I need to explain it. We must first look carefully at the exact situation.

Tigger is availing himself of Kanga's invitation and investigating the resources of her larder. Kanga herself, Christopher Robin and Piglet are watching Roo have his Extract of Malt. Surveying the scene, Pooh realizes that his prediction of Kanga's generous welcome is being fulfilled. Further, he can predict that when Tigger has found nothing to his liking in Kanga's cupboard, his attention will be attracted to the little group round Roo. Just as Pooh knows intuitively that Tigger will not like condensed milk, it is plausible to assume that a similar intuition tells him that Tigger will like Extract of Malt.

He can therefore justifiably relax and enjoy his elevenses, while, no doubt, keeping a benevolent eye on proceedings.

## How not to interrupt a tin of condensed milk

It is easy enough once again to dismiss the absurd accusation of greed, but acute readers have often been puzzled by the last word in the paragraph we have been analysing. We read that Pooh took the 'small tin of condensed milk' into a corner 'to see that nobody interrupted *it*' (my emphasis). Why 'it' instead of the 'him' we probably expected? What does it mean to interrupt a tin of condensed milk?

It might be suggested that 'it' here means Pooh's elevenses or his enjoyment of the milk. Despite its superficial plausibility, this explanation does not stand up to close analysis. Milne's grammar is impeccable even when judged by strict traditional standards. The pronoun 'it' cannot here represent anything except 'a small tin of condensed milk'. Even apart from this insuperable objection, interpreting 'it' as elevenses lacks the depth we have learnt to expect in every detail of the Pooh opus.

As my more perceptive readers have already divined, the explanation lies in the symbolic meaning and associations of milk. 'The milk of human kindness', 'a land flowing with milk and honey' – these well known phrases remind us of the long-standing history of milk as a symbol of spiritual and emotional as well as of material sustenance. Honey has similar associations. The fact that Winnie-the-Pooh sustains himself on these foods which are both spiritually and materially nourishing, shows him an exemplar of that great tradition that refuses to regard the spiritual and the material as mutually exclusive.

So far, so good. The deep meaning of milk in this context is now clear. But there is still the question, What does it mean to interrupt milk? And why is Pooh so careful to ensure that nobody does interrupt it? We have already seen that he had already set up the situation that would lead to the solution of Tigger's immediate problem. He knew that Tigger would try Roo's Extract of Malt and find '*that's* what Tiggers like'. But finding suitable food for Tigger, urgent and important though it is, cannot not be the main aim of Pooh as psychologist. That surely is to help Tigger to curb his excessive bounciness while retaining his admirable vitality and spirit of adventure.

Kanga, the most perceptive of the Forest dwellers after Pooh himself, has a vital role to play in this. It is essential that she should play this role entirely in her own way. One of Pooh's greatest qualities is his ability to stand back and allow others to play their part. Thus the true milk of psychotherapeutic kindness sometimes lay in an apparently passive watchfulness. To appeal for his advice at this moment, however natural, would be to interrupt the true –

and effective – kindness by which he is letting Kanga and Tigger form the relationship that will have the major direct influence on Tigger's psyche. In passing, we should notice that this milk is *condensed*: that is, Pooh is exercising his kindness in a powerfully concentrated form.

The correctness of Pooh's judgement is confirmed at the end of the chapter when we read that Tigger 'always lived at Kanga's house afterwards, and had Extract of Malt for breakfast, dinner, and tea. And sometimes, when Kanga thought he wanted strengthening, he had a spoonful or two of Roo's breakfast after meals as medicine.'

## Kanga confides Roo to Tigger

When Tigger appears next it is, at Kanga's choosing, as a companion and, to an important degree – surely, given Roo's youth – as a guardian for Roo: 'She had sent them out with a packet of watercress sandwiches for Roo and

a packet of Extract-of-Malt sandwiches for Tigger, to have a nice long morning in the Forest not getting into mischief.'

All true Ursinologists will remember that Tigger proclaims that 'Tiggers are . . .' Strorny good flyers', who can fly as well as Owl . . . 'only they don't want to'; 'can jump as far as Kangas . . . when they want to'; and 'Of course they can [swim]. Tiggers can do everything.' Finally he says, 'Climbing trees is what they do best.'

Perhaps Tigger's experience with different kinds of food has taught him the danger of sweeping statements. For we learn almost immediately that 'of all the things which he had said Tiggers could do, the only one he felt really certain about suddenly was climbing trees.' And he proceeds to justify this claim.

Here we see his tendency to excessive optimism, his exuberance, both physical and temperamental. We have already seen that he is the reverse of introspective, and he is highly responsive to external stimuli: mirrors, tablecloths, honey, haycorns, thistles and Extract of Malt. All this evidence fits him admirably into the category Jung labelled 'extravert sensation'. Jung divided all people into two basic types: extraverted and introverted. These he calls 'attitude-types'. Tigger clearly fulfils Jung's criterion of an extravert. 'The extravert . . . has a positive relation to the object. He affirms its importance to such an extent that his subjective attitude is constantly related to and oriented by the object.' Jung further classified both these types according to what he called their function-types. Functions in this sense were Thinking, Feeling, Sensation, and Intuition. We cannot doubt that Tigger's dominant function is Sensation. As Jung says, 'He [the extraverted sensation type] is by no means unlovable; on the contrary, his lively capacity for enjoyment makes him very good company; he is usually a jolly fellow.'

The episode of tree-climbing supplies further evidence of Tigger's outward-looking character and responsiveness to the stimuli of the outer world. Though Tigger judges his climbing ability correctly, he does not foresee the difficulty of descending. So he and Roo have to wait aloft until Christopher Robin and Eeyore join Pooh and Piglet, who were already installed at the bottom of the tree. Christopher Robin has a bright idea:

'I'll take off my tunic and we'll each hold a corner, and then Roo and Tigger can jump into it, and it will be all soft and bouncy for them, and they won't hurt themselves.'

Roo performs his part with delight, and turns Christopher Robin's tunic into a prototypical trampoline. When it is Tigger's turn to jump, he faces a significant problem. His superior sensation function makes him keenly aware of the possible dangers of the jump. Characteristically, he envisages this in terms of category: 'It's all very well for Jumping Animals like Kangas, but it's quite different for Swimming Animals like Tiggers.' And he takes refuge in a daydream of floating and swimming. His problem is solved when a branch breaks under his weight. He falls to the ground and feels 'Bouncy again already'.

Now this episode is a particularly remarkable example of Winnie-the-Pooh's special contribution to psychotherapeutic technique. It is so original that it calls for some comment. Perhaps also for some explanation, as its originality may make it opaque to an uninstructed reader, who may find it puzzling in several ways. Let us itemize these.

## Pooh as the (almost) invisible therapist

1. Pooh appears to play only a minimal part, and that a physical, not a psychological one: holding one corner of the tunic for the treed pair to jump into.
2. When he and Piglet approach the tree, he says that Tigger and Roo are 'Jagulars', Fierce Animals that 'hide in the branches of trees and drop on you as you go underneath'.
3. When Tigger and Roo have identified themselves and explained their predicament, Pooh's response is to ask Piglet what they should do, and to start eating Tigger's sandwiches.

4. When Piglet asks whether Pooh could climb up to them, Pooh answers:

> 'I might, Piglet, and I might bring Roo down on my back, but I couldn't bring Tigger down. So we must think of something else.' And in a thoughtful way he began to eat Roo's sandwiches, too.

5. Tigger's rashness in taking Roo up the tree which neither could descend casts grave doubt on Kanga's discretion in entrusting her precious Roo to Tigger's care. This, in turn, casts doubt on Pooh's judgement in choosing Kanga as Tigger's surrogate mother.

All true Ursinologists will be confident that these objections can be satisfactorily answered. But even they may feel explanations are needed. These it is my pleasant duty to supply.

The answer to the first objection will appear obvious and inevitable when the others have dealt with. So we will turn to them.

2. Most Ursinologists will have solved this problem for themselves. 'Jagulars' are patently just one of Pooh's jokes. He probably hoped that, after the example of the equally imaginary 'Heffalump', Piglet would realize this. This interpretation is supported by strong internal evidence. It is intrinsically improbable that Pooh, with his Enormous Brain, would believe in the existence of an animal

unknown to zoological science. He gives us a further clue
when he cites his authority for such a belief: "Christopher
Robin told me.' We have both negative and positive
evidence for discounting Christopher Robin's opinion in
such matters. In the final chapter of *The House at Pooh
Corner*, he gives Pooh a long and varied list of what he has
been learning. This contains nothing about Natural
History in any form. Strong negative evidence against
taking his statements on the subject seriously. As a positive
disqualification, we remember that it was he who claimed
he had seen a Heffalump.

3. It is a moot point whether Pooh really hoped that Piglet
would come up with a possible or even an interesting
solution. As for his eating Tigger's sandwiches, it should be
unnecessary to defend him yet again from the charge of
greed. A moment's reflection will remind us that
sandwiches left too long become unpalatable. Pooh was
preventing Kanga's sandwiches from being wasted.

We can be sure Kanga would have approved. Moreover,
Pooh could foresee that when Tigger and Roo did come
back to earth, they would inevitably be in a state of some
tension. Eating in such a state would probably cause
indigestion. So in the simple act of eating sandwiches
Pooh was preventing waste, protecting his friends' health
and sustaining his own powers.

4. Pooh shows his habitual firm grasp of reality when he
admits he could not bring Tigger down: 'So we must think

of something else,' he says. The 'something else', of course, was Christopher Robin's plan. Pooh himself could not execute this, (a) because, unlike Christopher Robin, he wore nothing that could function as a safety net, (b) even if he had such a garment, it would have needed two more people to hold the corners. But can we suppose for a moment that he had not foreseen that Christopher Robin and Eeyore would arrive and give precisely the help that was needed? This is another example of therapeutic originality in making use of his friends' particular abilities.

5. Similarly, just as Kanga had been rightly confident that Roo would come to no harm when he had been kidnapped, she was now equally confident that Tigger's rashness would delight Roo without endangering him. There is no explicit evidence that she felt this confidence because she knew Pooh was keeping benevolent watch over all. But the close rapport that had developed between them makes this interpretation highly plausible.

Thus we have not only answered all the other separate objections, but we now see that their cumulative effect also answers the first and fundamental objection. Far from playing a mere, and non-psychological, supporting role, Pooh was the guiding spirit in the whole affair. It was, in fact, a supreme example of that original methodology we have referred to: using his friends to play roles vital to treatment he was carrying out. This, as I am sure you realize, had a double value. It was psychologically beneficial to his – unconscious – assistants as well as to the more obvious object of his treatment.

His own willingness to appear a mere auxiliary built up their confidence, gave them the pleasing experience of active benevolence, and, of course, bore further testimony to Pooh's exemplary modesty.

Before we go on to complete the fascinating case study of Tigger, I must admit I owe a little more explanation to my readers. Some of you may feel that for once I have departed from that strict adherence to empirical evidence that has hitherto characterized all my Ursinological studies. Where, you may ask, are the indubitable facts that show Pooh as the firm though unobtrusive author and director of this little drama?

I must confess that these are not unreasonable questions. I must even admit that not all of them can be answered as fully and concretely as one would like. I hope, however, that fair-minded enquirers will in their turn admit that this is inevitable in the nature of the case. It is in the very nature of Pooh's indirect and self-effacing approach that it does not leave blatant and conspicuous traces.

How then, you will ask, can I justify my interpretation? Let us remember that the good and wise Bishop Butler (in his *Analogy of Religion*, 1736) taught us that probability is the guide to life. When we estimate the probability of an explanation of a particular event, we are bound to consider that event, not in isolation, but in relation to surrounding events and to the characters involved. I would maintain that the wise bishop's principles lead us to an unqualified acceptance of Pooh's leading role in the otherwise inexplicable incident of Tigger, Roo and the pine tree.

I hope also that my frankness in pointing out these issues will render my other interpretations all the more obviously scientific and convincing.

## Tigger and Eeyore

Tigger's next appearance shows some interesting new behaviour, illustrating once again the nuanced subtlety of Milne's masterpiece. The full title of the relevant chapter is 'In which Pooh invents a new game and Eeyore joins in'. Leaving aside the manifold riches of its early pages, we come to the point where Eeyore complains he has been BOUNCED into the river, and Piglet suggests that Tigger had been the bouncer. At that moment Tigger appears and is accused of the bouncing.

His normal cheerfulness turns to discomfort, prevarication and defensive crossness. That is, he shows all the signs of guilt. Different schools of psychology assign different causes to guilt. Psychoanalytic theories ascribe it to internalized prohibitions imposed by early authority figures. But there is no evidence that such figures had ever existed in Tigger's experience. This also disqualifies behaviourist theories which regard guilt as a conditioned response to actions that have led to punishment in the past. Much more applicable seem existentialist theories that view guilt as a reaction to behaviour that hinders the realization of one's full potential.

From this point of view, Tigger is suffering two causes of guilt. His action in bouncing Eeyore impedes his wish to be friends with everybody, yet any veto on such bouncing hinders his natural exuberance. No wonder he comes as near as his nature permits to existentialist *angst*!

Fortunately help is at hand. Once again we see Pooh's wise passiveness allowing Christopher Robin to relieve the tension by proposing a game of Poohsticks. Then Eeyore himself finally goes off with Tigger, telling him how to win at Poohsticks. It would be neurotically sceptical to doubt that when Pooh invented Poohsticks he foresaw its use in therapy. We are reminded of Winnicott's ideas in, *Playing and Reality*. In that he was primarily concerned with play of mother with child but it does not seem excessive to extrapolate to the extent of applying his 'Thus the way is paved for playing together in a relationship' to the happier relationship of Eeyore with Tigger.

Yet again we witnesss Pooh's unique methodology of guiding Tigger and Eeyore into a highly successful therapeutic interaction. In our next case we shall examine his use of Behavioural Therapy to cure Rabbit's bossiness. All we need say about it now is that it triumphantly vindicates his refusal to destroy Tigger's innate liveliness while guiding it into acceptable channels.

## Case 4

### The problems of Rabbit

From his very first appearance, there is a fundamental ambiguity in the character of Rabbit. He receives warm praise and the honour of frequent visits from Winnie-the-Pooh. On the other hand, he often appears excessively bossy, 'Captainish' in Milne's superbly chosen term. So we shall first analyse him as an example of Adorno's authoritarian personality, and then look for the roots of this personality, which Pooh will identify as an Adlerian inferiority complex. We must also continually balance the less attractive sides of his character with those traits that made him worthy of Pooh's friendship. Finally, we shall draw these superficially contradictory traits together by showing how Pooh first understands Rabbit's problems, and then solves them by applying varied psychological approaches.

As we follow this intricate and complex case study, we shall appreciate not only Pooh's wide knowledge but also the exquisite tact with which he helps and guides without imposing. We note particularly how he uses his insight into his friends' characters to produce interactions which combine their free choices with his overall guidance to reach a happy conclusion.

The behaviour of many eminent psychologists has led us to expect a more proactive form of therapy and a stance of superiority to their clients. We may, therefore, be inclined to forgive those who have failed to recognize Pooh's masterly skill because of its very subtlety. Nowhere is this better demonstrated than in the case of Rabbit. First though let us examine the nature of Rabbit's psychological problems.

## Rabbit as an authoritarian personality

Milne gives us the key to these problems when he calls Rabbit 'Captainish': thus clearly indicating authoritarian personality traits. I hope it is not necessary to argue at length that even authoritarian traits find only very mild expression in the happy, idyllic world of Pooh. Milne, however, was too great a realist to be unaware of more serious aspects of these problems. Though obliquely presented, they are there for the perceptive reader to notice.

Adorno's most famous work on the subject, *The Authoritarian Personality*, lists some of the following as typical authoritarian personality traits:

A tendency to be on the lookout for, and to condemn, reject and punish people who violate conventional values.

A rigid adherence to conventional, middle-class values.

A preoccupation with the dominance—submission, strong—weak, leader—follower dimension.

The disposition to believe that wild and dangerous things go on in the world.

All of these we shall find in Rabbit. Let us, thus alerted, now look at the particular examples.

### The judgemental Rabbit

In the second chapter of Winnie-the-Pooh, Pooh comes to a large hole in a sandy bank.

'Aha!' said Pooh. (*Rum-tum-tiddle-um-tum.*) 'If I know anything about anything, that hole means Rabbit,' he said, 'and Rabbit means Company,' he said, and Company means Food and Listening-to-Me-Humming and such like. *Rum-tum-tum-tiddle-um.*'

Rabbit's hospitality is so generous that when Pooh tries to leave, he gets stuck in the doorway and becomes 'A Wedged Bear in Great Tightness'. We have already dealt with the true significance of Pooh's situation in Chapter I, so now let us concentrate on Rabbit's behaviour.

Hitherto Rabbit's conduct had fully justified Pooh's favourable predictions. Now, though, his tone becomes censorious:

'It all comes,' said Rabbit sternly, 'of eating too much. I thought at the time,' said Rabbit, 'only I didn't like to say anything,' said Rabbit, that one of us was eating too much,' said Rabbit, 'and I knew it wasn't *me*,' he said.

Remembering the character traits in Adorno's list, we notice Rabbit's quickness to note and condemn what he judges to be Pooh's over-eating. His strict adherence to conventional, middle-class values is illustrated by his superficially polite refusal to comment on Pooh's over-eating when it would have seemed helpful to do so. His self-righteous denial of any guilt on his part is also typical of the type we are studying. 'Their descriptions of themselves have a definitely moralistic tone.'

With regard to the accusation of gluttony, we have already refuted the all too prevalent but manifestly absurd notion that this incident shows Pooh as greedy. As we now know, he was simply *demonstrating* the dangers of excess, even at the expense of his own comfort and dignity. Yet another proof that Pooh was one who, as a Buddhist sage recommended, 'had renounced conceit'. And Pooh reaped the promised reward of being free from all bonds. An example that some other psychologists could follow with benefit to themselves and others.

We must not be too severe on Rabbit's misjudgement. We cannot fairly blame him for an error shared by all until the recent researches of devoted Ursinologists. But it is harder to excuse his manner. The text tells us that he spoke 'sternly': an unusual attitude in the Pooh opus. It is, of course, typical of the authoritarian manner.

## A stereotypical in-group reaction to an out-group

When Kanga and Baby Roo first appear in the Forest, Rabbit's first reaction is hostile. This key passage must be quoted at length, before we analyse it in detail.

> 'What I don't like about it is this,' said Rabbit. 'Here we are — you, Pooh, and you, Piglet, and Me — and suddenly —
> 'And Eeyore,' said Pooh.
> And Eeyore — and then suddenly —'
> 'And Owl,' said Pooh.
> 'And Owl — and then all of a sudden —'

'Oh, and Eeyore,' said Pooh. 'I was forgetting *him*.'

'Here – we – are,' said Rabbit very slowly and carefully, 'all – of – us, and then, suddenly, we wake up one morning, and what do we find? An animal of whom we have never even heard before! An animal who carries her family about with her in her pocket!'

He goes on to propose a plan for disposing of these – to him – unwelcome intruders:

'The best way . . . would be to steal Baby Roo and hide him, and then when Kanga says, "Where's Baby Roo?" we say "Aha!" . . . so that Kanga knows that we know where Baby Roo is. 'Aha!' means "We'll tell you where Baby Roo is, if you promise to go away from the Forest and never come back."'

Rabbit's main objections to Kanga and Roo may be listed as follows:

1. Kanga and Roo are newcomers.
2. They have never been heard of before.
3. They are intrinsically odd.
4. They do not belong to any recognized category.
5. They are intruders on a well established group.

Here we have a classic case of the hostile way in which an established in-group all too often reacts to an out-group, especially when the in-group reaction is expressed by an authoritarian representative. Readers of the late Henri Tajfel's *Human Groups and Social Categories* will have noticed that Rabbit displays all three of the components that may characterize a group. Tajfel listed these (in Part I, Ch. 2) as (i) a cognitive component; (ii) an evaluative component; (iii) an emotional component.

1. Rabbit displays the cognitive component when he says, 'Here we are . . . all of us.' This indicates his knowledge of belonging to a group and the complementary emphasis on the defining contrast with the out-group.
2. He then makes a value judgement of his (in)–group compared with the out-group – Kanga and Roo.
3. Finally, we have the emotional component; here evinced by a hostility so strong that it leads him to propose kidnapping Roo, by far the most violent act in the whole Pooh saga.

Rabbit is also uneasy with Kanga's carrying Roo in what he calls her 'pocket'. This clearly implies sexist prejudice, a trait that typically accompanies the authoritarian personality we have already recognized in Rabbit.

Now we must carefully note Pooh's responses to Rabbit. First of all, he widens the group. Rabbit had mentioned only those members who were physically present: Pooh and Piglet. Pooh reminds him of Owl and Eeyore. Curiously he mentions Eeyore twice, adding, after the second mention, 'I was forgetting him.' Even those who still adhere to the exploded myth that Pooh was really a Bear of Very Little

Brain can hardly believe he would have forgotten the first mention quite so soon. What then is the true explanation?

Obviously he wants to make Rabbit realize that he was forgetting even the other members of his own group. Perhaps Pooh also suspects that Rabbit may not regard the reclusive Eeyore as a full member of the in-group. In any case, he uses the pretence of having himself forgotten to make his point without offending Rabbit. For Rabbit, like most sufferers from an inferiority complex, was ultra-sensitive to criticism. Just as typically, he is quite insensitive to the feelings of others. Thus, when Pooh remarks that they could say 'Aha!' even if they hadn't stolen Baby Roo, 'Pooh,' said Rabbit kindly, 'you haven't any brain.'

Pooh's answer 'I know' means, of course, that he had not got a brain at all like Rabbit's. He is obliquely but unmistakably implying the fundamental wrongheadedness of Rabbit's whole response. Rabbit's rejoinder displays that sort of arrogant obtuseness that Nietzsche commented on when he said 'power makes *stupid*'. The fact that he spoke 'kindly' does credit to his basic good nature but none to his intelligence.

Rabbit's elaborate, numbered tabulation of his plan displays a characteristic urge to exercise detailed control over events and persons. Linked with his sexist attitude to Kanga, this also shows what Adler described 'an overstrained desire for masculinity . . . a will to conquer all difficulties of life in the masculine fashion'.

Yet the better side of his nature is highlighted when we learn almost immediately after the kidnapping that 'Rabbit was playing with Baby Roo in his own house, and feeling more fond of him every minute'. Nor was this fondness a passing whim, for, at the end of the chapter we read 'And every Tuesday Roo spent with his great friend Rabbit . . .'

Moreover, in Chapter Four of *The House at Pooh Corner* we meet a high tribute to Rabbit from the Great Bear himself. A tribute which also reiterates his preference for plain English.

'I like talking to Rabbit. He talks about sensible things . . .
He uses short, easy words, like "What about lunch?" and
"Help yourself, Pooh."'

Which made him think of another verse:

Oh, I like his way of talking,
    Yes, I do.
It's the nicest way of talking
    Just for two.
And a Help-yourself with Rabbit
Though it may become a habit,
Is a *pleasant* sort of habit
    For a Pooh.

This should fix two important judgements in our minds. First and obviously, Pooh's warmly favourable opinion of Rabbit. Second, the important limitation clearly stated in the second and third lines. These tell us that Rabbit is at his best in a duologue. And not in any duologue, but one with Pooh Bear. Here there is a clear negative implication that Rabbit might not appear to such advantage in other company. Remember his dismissive catalogue of the other Forest dwellers in 'Rabbit's busy day'. In his judgement, Pooh, Piglet and Eeyore are brainless; Owl's ability to spell Tuesday is often irrelevant; Kanga is too preoccupied with Roo; Roo is too young; Tigger too bouncy. 'So there's really nobody but Me, when you come to look at it.'

It is not surprising then to find that the happy ending of the kidnapping incident does not mean that Rabbit's problems were all solved. It is indeed a tribute to Milne's profound realism that he reminds us that psychotherapists must be prepared for disappointments and relapses; and this applies even to Winnie-the-Pooh. Moreover, a success may contain the seeds of future trouble. Thus Rabbit's genuine friendliness to Baby Roo is partly based on the fact that Roo ministers to his self-esteem: he 'said "Yes, Rabbit" and "No, Rabbit" almost better than anybody else in the Forest.' Inevitably this desire to dominate makes Rabbit uneasy with Tigger. This situation calls forth all Pooh's skill as a psychologist.

## The cure of Rabbit's Tigger phobia

All Ursinologists are familiar with the episode in *The House at*

*Pooh Corner* entitled 'In which Tigger is unbounced'. Here Rabbit's bossiness and his distaste for Tigger's superabundant vitality join in his attempt to unbounce Tigger by taking him on 'a long explore' and losing him till next morning. By that time, Rabbit predicts, 'he'll be a Humble Tigger . . . a Sad Tigger, a Melancholy Tigger, a Small and Sorry Tigger, an Oh-Rabbit-I-am-glad-to-see-you Tigger.'

Here Rabbit blatantly proclaims his intolerance of Tigger's free vitality and his desire to reduce him to humble docility: again a typically authoritarian attitude.

Rabbit tries to cure Tigger's bounciness by associating it with the unpleasant experience of being alone and lost in the Forest mist. This technique is often called 'punishment', but perhaps the more neutral term 'negative reinforcement' is preferable. Rabbit's attempt misfires, because Rabbit himself gets lost and is eventually rescued by his intended subject, Tigger.

> And at last a very Small and Sorry Rabbit heard him [Tigger]. And the Small and Sorry Rabbit rushed through the mist at the noise, and it suddenly turned into Tigger; a Friendly Tigger, a Grand Tigger, a Large and Helpful Tigger, a Tigger who bounced, if he bounced at all, in just the beautiful way a Tigger ought to bounce.

As our more experienced readers have doubtless perceived, the previous paragraph is far from exhausting the psychological significance of this episode. Though

Rabbit's attempt at therapy failed, it did indicate his own ambition to become a therapist. Pooh Bear is aware both of the ambition and the root cause of its failure. Rabbit failed because he was primarily concerned to impose his own standards of behaviour on Tigger. Over and over again we notice how careful Pooh is to avoid this dictatorial approach to psychotherapy. His aim always is to help his clients to help themselves and to achieve psychic health in their own way. Though rejecting Rabbit's Captainish attitude, he welcomes his desire to help his friends. He succeeds so well in this that, as we shall see, he enlists Rabbit's help in the treatment of Eeyore. If not quite a therapist, Rabbit ends by being at least a counsellor.

The mere story of Rabbit and Tigger is so enthralling that generations of readers have overlooked the subtle way in which Winnie-the-Pooh guided the whole affair and brought about the happy ending. Let us now study this case again, this time focusing our analysis on Pooh, on all he says and does and on all that he significantly does not say and do.

## Pooh's diagnosis

Now we now come to the really important question: what was Winnie-the-Pooh's attitude throughout this incident? How did he diagnose Rabbit's psychological problem? How did he treat it? The key passage occurs in Chapter Seven of *The House at Pooh Corner*, 'In which Tigger is unbounced'. All familiar with the canonical text will remember that while Rabbit is unfolding his plan to

Unbounce Tigger, Pooh has got into 'a comfortable position for not listening to Rabbit'. Yet,
just as we should expect, he immediately seizes the nub of Rabbit's problem. When Rabbit says about Tigger, 'There's too much of him . . . that's what it comes to,' Pooh hums quietly to himself:

> If Rabbit
> Was bigger
> And fatter
> And stronger,
> Or bigger
> Than Tigger,
> If Tigger was smaller,
> Then Tigger's bad habit
> Of bouncing at Rabbit
> Would matter
> No longer,
> If Rabbit
> Was taller.

Pooh's infallible diagnostic skill recognizes a classic case of Alfred Adler's picture of an inferiority complex. In the 1920s, when the Pooh papers were first published, Adler's Individual Psychology was as well known as Freud's Psychoanalysis or Jung's Analytical Psychology. Even now, his concept of the inferiority complex is well known, though he himself has been largely forgotten until recent signs of revived interest.

In Adlerian terms, Rabbit's smaller size makes him feel inferior to any larger animal: to Kanga, to Eeyore, to Pooh himself, but most of all to the large and Bouncy Tigger. Typically, Rabbit tries to compensate for this by his domineering, 'Captainish' behaviour. This reaches a climax in the attempt to Unbounce Tigger.

Pooh's earlier awareness of the situation explained his attitude during Rabbit's plan for expelling Kanga and Roo.

Indirectly, but clearly enough to any perceptive observer, Pooh indicated his sceptical detachment from Rabbit's scheme. Rightly confident that no harm would ensue, he let things take their course – another example of his settled policy of allowing his friends to learn as much as possible for themselves. He may even have hoped that Rabbit's friendship with Roo would buttress his self-confidence and so make him more tolerant. As we have just seen, this was true only up to a point. Of course, Tigger had not then appeared, and he posed a greater threat to Rabbit's precarious psyche. Precarious though it was, it had clearly improved from the time where he wanted to expel Kanga and Roo. Now he wants only to tame Tigger.

## Pooh sees the way to treat Rabbit

At first, Pooh seems to be repeating the approach he used so successfully in the case of Kanga and Roo. Benevolent detachment is the common factor. But now the text gives us a clearer hint that Pooh is in control, however unobtrusive that control may be. Rabbit has just expounded his plan to unbounce Tigger by taking him on a long explore to the North Pole and losing him there.

> It was now Pooh's turn to feel very glad, because it was he who had first found the North Pole, and when they got there, Tigger would see a notice which said, 'Discovered by Pooh, Pooh found it', and then Tigger would know, which perhaps he didn't now, the sort of Bear Pooh was. *That* sort of Bear.

Now earlier researches have already disclosed a few of the multiple meanings of the North Pole in an Ursinian context. To its representation of philosophical truth in *Pooh and the Philosophers* and a successful Arthurian quest in *Pooh and the Ancient Mysteries*, we can now add its function as a symbol of the journey to psychic health.

An objection may arise here. Some readers may point out (a) that we have no evidence that Tigger reached the North Pole, and (b) that in any case it was not his but Rabbit's psyche that needed cure. Though it is always pleasing to find readers exercising a properly critical attitude, we must protest when we meet criticisms that are hasty or superficial or over literal. Or, as now, all three.

The apparent problems disappear when we look at the quoted paragraph in its context, and not merely in its immediate but in its wider context. Viewed thus, we see at once that Pooh is glad, indeed *very* glad, because he has now found the way to restore Rabbit to psychic health. Tigger himself is not Pooh's problem at the moment. He has handed that to Kanga, who, as we have already seen, is being remarkably successful in socializing Tigger. Happily domesticated with her and Roo, he has, despite the 'boffing' episode, made friends with Eeyore. Admittedly, Rabbit remains unreconciled, but, as this chapter so dramatically demonstrates, the true solution is not to unbounce Tigger but to persuade Rabbit to see his bounciness as natural and admirable. An excellent example of what Professor Ellen Langer tells us of the liberating effect of a new point of view.

In therapeutic terms, this is precisely what Pooh has discovered, and proceeds to put into practice.

## From diagnosis to treatment

As with the plan to kidnap Roo, Pooh combines outward co-operation with unmistakable detachment. He also gives several warning hints that anyone less self-absorbed than Rabbit would have picked up. E. H. Shepard's illustration showing the group setting out in the mist gives a graphic message. Rabbit, who is leading, looks over his shoulder

and clearly establishes eye-contact with Pooh. Pooh's expression would have given a wiser Rabbit pause for thought. But Rabbit presses on regardless.

Tigger at this point runs on ahead of the others. On Rabbit's command, they hide in a hollow beside the path. When Tigger has been gone for some time, 'Rabbit got up and stretched himself'.

'Well?' he whispered proudly. 'There we are! Just as I said.'
   'I've been thinking,' said Pooh, 'and I think —
   'No,' said Rabbit. 'Don't. Run. Come on.'

We Ursinologists must feel deeply shocked every time we read this passage. To interrupt the Great Bear when he was about to announce his latest thought shows Rabbit plumbing the depths of arrogant deafness to the voice of wisdom. He does then raise our hopes for a moment, only to dash them:

'Now,' said Rabbit, after they had gone a little way, 'we can talk. What were you going to say, Pooh?'
   'Nothing much. Why are we going along here?'
   'Because it's the way home.'
   'Oh!' said Pooh.

This brief but pregnant dialogue reminds us of the vital importance of punctuation in the great Milnean texts. The question mark after Pooh's question, though obviously correct, might be considered merely the conventional sign after a normally formed question. But the exclamation mark after 'Oh' tells us that it was not a neutral 'Oh' indicating mere acknowledgement of Rabbit's statement and perhaps agreement with it. On the contrary, it expresses surprise, even astonishment. In the context, it is a virtual contradiction of Rabbit's assertion that they were on the right track for home. Yet Rabbit completely ignores it.

It grows more and more obvious that Rabbit has lost his way. By now, we can hardly fail to be impressed by the repeated emphasis on mist. The function of weather is yet another aspect of the Pooh saga which has been grossly neglected. What does the text tell us about the weather on the day of Tigger's Unbouncing? 'The next day was quite a different day. Instead of being hot and sunny, it was cold and misty.' Can we doubt that this mist symbolized the mental confusion in which Rabbit lost his way, psychologically as well as physically?

With admirable patience, Pooh gives Rabbit chance after chance to recognize the truth. His own grasp of the truth is made clear.

> Pooh was getting rather tired of that sand-pit, and suspected it of following them about, because whichever direction they started in, they always ended

up at it, and each time, as it came through the mist at them, Rabbit said triumphantly, 'Now I know where we are!' and Pooh said sadly, 'So do I.'

The psychological significance of the pit seems to have gone unrecognized. All who have read 'He that diggeth a pit shall fall into it' (*Ecclesiastes*, x, 8) will recognize that a pit is a traditional symbol for a trap, and in this sense it tells us that Rabbit cannot escape from the psychological trap he has fallen into.

When Pooh says 'So do I' he is recognizing the truth, and he says it sadly because it shows Rabbit is still failing to do so. Pooh then suggests that they should walk out of sight of the pit and then try to find it again. He explains:

'Well, we keep looking for Home and not finding it, so I thought if we looked for this Pit, we'd be sure not to find it, which would be a Good Thing, because then we might find something that we *weren't* looking for, which might be just what we *were* looking for, really.'

'I don't see much sense in that,' said Rabbit.

'No,' said Pooh humbly, 'there isn't. But there was *going* to be when I began it. It's just that something happened to it on the way.'

What happened, of course, was Rabbit's stubborn incomprehension which blocked the way from Pooh's words to Rabbit's understanding. The leading exponent of

Social Skills, Professor Michael Argyle, has pointed out that the proper *receiving* of messages needs training as much as the proper sending of them. Pooh, of course, has told us this already. And in a situation involving Rabbit.

When Rabbit was planning to expel Kanga and Roo from the Forest, he said that when they kidnapped Roo, they would go to Kanga and say, 'Aha!' This, he explained, means 'We'll tell you where Baby Roo is if you promise to go away from the Forest and never come back.' Pooh thinks, 'I wonder if Kanga will have to practise so as to understand it.'

The psychology of Social Skills does provide a good explanation of Rabbit's deafness to Pooh's wisdom. But an even more important and wide-ranging psychological explanation is reserved for the summing-up at the end of this little book.

Despite his incomprehension, Rabbit does try Pooh's experiment. Naturally, he verifies Pooh's prediction by failing to return to the pit. Before moving on to Pooh's next step, we need to examine the previous quotation in detail. Pooh's suggestion that they might find the way home by looking for the sand-pit, is, of course, a simple, concrete example of the indirect approach that he employs time and again in his therapeutic practice.

## Brilliant success of Pooh's treatment

The tender-hearted reader may feel that Pooh was being rather unkind in leaving the lost Rabbit alone in the mist. Such a reader must trust in Pooh's wisdom, and be comfortably certain that Pooh knew that only a painful experience would enable Rabbit to see Tigger no longer as a dangerous threat, but as a powerful rescuer.

Nowhere is Pooh's therapeutic success more eloquently expressed than in the last lines of of Chapter Eight of *The House at Pooh Corner:*

> And the Small and Sorry Rabbit rushed through the mist at the noise, and it suddenly turned into Tigger; a Friendly Tigger, a Grand Tigger, a Large and Helpful Tigger, a Tigger who bounced, if he bounced at all, in just the beautiful way a Tigger ought to bounce.

Once again, Pooh's approach to Rabbit's problem was thoroughly eclectic. His diagnosis of Rabbit's inferiority complex was Adlerian. The treatment was straightforwardly behavioural. The painful experience of being lost and alone in the misty Forest stimulated desire to avoid repetition. The rescue by Tigger not only gave overwhelming relief and pleasure but associated these feelings with Tigger. This in turn led to a cognitive change in his perception of Tigger. He now saw Tigger as a friendly rescuer instead of as an over bouncy menace.

Just as Pooh brought Rabbit to accept Tigger's bounciness as an admirable part of his nature, so Pooh saw that Rabbit's Captainishness was by no means wholly bad. A better balanced Rabbit had indeed much to offer the Forest community. At the end of *The House at Pooh Corner*, it is Rabbit who organizes the Rissolution to mark Christopher Robin's departure. He 'brained out a Notice', one typical of his prose style, but socially acceptable in content and purpose.

Not only is Rabbit now making good use of his organizing skills, he plays a vital role in bringing Eeyore into social activity. In one of the most astonishing reversals of psychological history, it is Eeyore who proposes the Rissolution in a poem of his own composition. This could hardly have happened merely at Rabbit's *invitation*. When we look back to the previous chapter, we find Rabbit visiting Eeyore and employing a form of cognitive therapy when Eeyore complains he lacks society.

'It's your fault, Eeyore. You've never been to see any of us. You just stay here in this one corner of the Forest waiting for others to come to *you*. Why don't you go to *them* sometimes?' Eeyore was silent for a little while, thinking. 'There may be something in what you say, Rabbit,' he said at last. 'I have been neglecting you. I must move about more. I must come and go.'

Can we doubt that Rabbit, the new, well balanced Rabbit, has constituted himself Pooh's assistant, that he is in fact a lay counsellor?

*Rabbit,*

## Case 5

## *Parenting: Kanga and Roo*

Pooh plays an exceptionally unobtrusive role in this case history. Recognizing the profound rightness of Kanga's parenting, he confines himself for the most part to benevolent watchfulness. His attitude implicitly warns other therapists against the temptation to take excessive control. In other words, what Pooh doesn't do is as therapeutically important as what he does.

Kanga and Roo present us with the only example of mother–child relations in the world of Pooh. It is an exceptionally happy relationship. As we shall see when we examine it in detail, this was the result of Kanga's precisely correct balance between protectiveness and freedom.

Kanga's mothering of Roo is naturally full of implicit references to Winnicott. Unlike so many psychoanalysts, he stresses the happy side of childhood rather than its traumas. In Roo's case, this is due mainly to Kanga's wisdom, but also, as we should expect, to the role of Pooh Bear. Let us examine both in turn.

## *Playing and reality in Roo's development*

Winnicott particularly stresses the importance of play in a child's development. Through play, Roo learns a series of vital lessons. First, he forms a loving but independent relationship with his mother. Then he recognizes external reality. Then he is abducted into a strange situation, where he faces a new and potentially frightening situation courageously. Finally, he enters happily into the varied society of the Forest.

The first definite fact we learn about Roo is that Kanga 'carries him about with her in her in her pocket'. The specially close relationship continues even when Roo is not actually in his mother's pouch. When Rabbit is making his kidnap plan, he admits that one difficulty is that 'Kanga never takes her eye off Baby Roo, except when he's safely buttoned up in her pocket.'

This is amply corroborated when Rabbit begins to put his plan into action. Rabbit, accompanied by the participating Piglet and the detachedly observing Pooh, finds 'Baby Roo was practising very small jumps in the sand, and falling down mouse-holes and climbing out of them . . .'. Note that this clearly implies that Roo recognizes the independent reality of the sand and the mouse-holes. This indicates he has passed beyond the stage when very young children are not, according to Jean Piaget, aware of themselves as separate from their environment. In the same scene, when Roo squeaked, 'Look at me jumping,' his 'me' indicates a further stage in self-awareness.

The text repeatedly emphasizes how difficult it is to distract Kanga's attention from Roo. Even a new poem composed and recited by Pooh himself does not shift her focus. Could single-minded concentration be more forcibly expressed?

Equally, however, we must notice that this scene indicates a step forward in Roo's advance to comparative independence. Though still protected by his mother's vigilance, he is playing vigorously, falling down mouse-holes and climbing out unaided and apparently unperturbed. This independent though supervised play must, according to Winnicott, have been preceded by playing with Kanga.

His confidence has now been built up so strongly that he shows no alarm when he has been kidnapped and is soon playing happily with Rabbit, his kidnapper. Only a child who had been given an unshakeable confidence could have reacted so fearlessly and cheerfully to such a strange experience. His reaction must have been in Professor Mary Ainsworth's mind when she wrote about children's use of their mother as a 'secure base' and inspired her investigations into infants' reactions to what is known as 'the strange situation'.

We note again the important function of play in his surprising rapport with Rabbit. We note also that another eminent child psychologist, John Bowlby (1907–1990), agrees with Ainsworth, saying that a child's ability to accept the mother's absence suggests that 'some maturational threshold is passed' (*Attachment*, p. 252).

It is worth commenting, I think, that Kanga shares this confidence.

Of course as soon as Kanga unbuttoned her pocket, she saw what had happened. Just for a moment, she thought she was frightened, and then she knew she wasn't; for she felt sure that Christopher Robin would never let any harm happen to Roo.

Her calm confidence extends to Roo's feelings. Not only is she sure that he will not suffer any harm; she seems equally sure he will not feel any painful anxiety. Far from reacting to the kidnapping with the ferocity that Piglet feared, she turns the whole thing into a joke. Admittedly, Piglet does not enjoy the joke when Kanga pretends not to notice that he has replaced Roo in her pouch, and gives the reluctant substitute a cold bath. No doubt he feels it is adding insult to injury when she says he must take his strengthening medicine because 'You don't want to grow up small and weak like Piglet, do you?'

### Roo matures further during the Expotition to the North Pole

Though he starts the Expotition in Kanga's pouch, after they have all eaten their Provisions we find 'Roo was washing his face and paws in the stream, while Kanga explained to everybody proudly that this was the first time he had ever washed his face himself . . .'

It was at this moment that Roo falls into the river. This time, Kanga does express anxiety, though this never reaches panic. But the striking thing is Roo's own reaction.

> 'Look at me swimming!' squeaked Roo from the middle
> of his pool, and was hurried down a waterfall into the
> next pool.

As the current swirls Roo from pool to pool, and all but one of his friends are rushing about, making well meaning but ineffectual efforts to rescue him, he himself continues to call happily, 'Look at me swimming!'

The one who is not fussing futilely is, of course, Winnie-the-Pooh. Sagaciously anticipating which pool Roo will arrive at, he, joined by Kanga, holds a long pole across the pool and Roo, still bubbling proudly, 'Look at me swimming', drifts up against it and climbs out.

## Pooh's role in Roo's maturation

Until this rescue, Pooh has played an unusually unobtrusive part in the development of Roo. Unobtrusive, but not uninfluential. While Rabbit is making his xenophobic plan to get rid of Kanga and Roo, Pooh's attitude is more than detached. His sceptical questions, totally misunderstood by the blinkered Rabbit, clearly imply that he considers the whole scheme both misguided and impracticable.

Lest Pooh's attitude to Kanga has been too subtly indicated, it is spelled out when we are told that Pooh 'had decided to be a Kanga'. If any reader had still failed to get the message, it is hammered home when we see that it was Kanga and Pooh *together* who rescued Roo.

So far, we have seen that Kanga began by giving Roo the protective care that built up his confidence. This confidence showed in his apparently untroubled reaction to being kidnapped, and in the way in which he converted the potentially frightening experience of falling into the stream to the triumphant experience of his first swim.

## Roo's entry into formal society

The last chapter of *Winnie-the-Pooh* displays an important further step in Roo's maturation. This chapter, you will remember, concerns the party that Christopher Robin gives in honour of Pooh's rescue of Piglet. 'It was the first party to which Roo had ever been, and he was very excited. As soon as ever they had sat down he began to talk.' In turn, he says 'Hallo' to the other guests, naturally – and significantly – beginning with Pooh.

The Pooh saga has sometimes been criticized as lacking in realism. Striking evidence to the contrary occurs just after Roo's socially poised greetings:

> Kanga said to Roo, 'Drink up your milk first, dear, and talk afterwards.' So Roo, who was drinking his milk, tried to say that he could do both at once . . . and had to be patted on the back and dried for quite a long time afterwards.

This very natural incident, and Roo's attack of hiccups later, show us that even Kanga's excellent mothering cannot prevent all minor accidents, and this touch of nature saves us from feeling that Roo is too good to be true. It should also encourage mothers not to blame themselves if their children do not always maintain impossible standards of perfection.

### Roo and Tigger

This profound psychological realism continues with Roo's development in *The House at Pooh Corner*. When Pooh and

Piglet take Tigger to Kanga's house, Roo greets all three in a manner that proves more than his obvious sociability and good manners. He might well have been frightened by the entry of this large and 'bouncy' stranger. But he shows not the slightest alarm, or even shyness. It is also interesting to note that he says 'Hallo, Pooh' and 'Hallo, Piglet' once each, but 'Hallo, Tigger' twice, because he had never said it before and it sounded funny'. This shows an increasing awareness of language and the first evidence we are given of his sense of humour.

Admittedly, Roo's humour is fairly rudimentary, based on the primitive feeling that the unfamiliar is intrinsically absurd. And he displays a similar relish of a comic situation when Tigger saves Roo from his hated Strengthening Medicine by 'gololloping' it himself.

> 'He's taken my medicine, he's taken my medicine, he's taken my medicine!' sang Roo happily, thinking it was a tremendous joke.

Another major step in Roo's maturation is described in the chapter entitled 'In which it is shown that Tiggers don't climb trees'. Hitherto, although Roo has had his adventures, they have been under Kanga's watchful eye. The one exception – Rabbit's kidnapping of Roo – was without her knowledge or consent. On the occasion we are now considering, she sent Roo off with Tigger 'to have a nice long morning in the Forest not getting into mischief'.

We must not for a moment suspect – no true

Ursinologist would suspect – that Kanga is wearying of her maternal responsibilities. The plain words of the text forbid any such misapprehension. The paragraph we have just looked at begins:

> Now it happened that Kanga had felt rather motherly that morning, and Wanting to Count Things – like Roo's vests, and how many pieces of soap there were left, and the two clean spots in Tigger's feeder.

There can really be no reasonable doubt as to how we should interpret this. It reminds us forcibly that the multifaceted work of motherhood unavoidably involves an important administrative element. Kanga also realizes that Roo and Tigger would be bored if they had to stay at home while she was busy Counting Things. Therefore she wisely provides them with healthy and tasty light refreshment and sends them off for a morning of fresh air and exercise.

Entrusting Roo to Tigger's care also exhibits gratifying – though not surprising – evidence that our text exhibits an exceptionally accurate anticipation of Bowlby. Too many readers have interpreted Bowlby as demanding that mothers should devote twenty-four hour care to their infant children. This in turn has led them to condemn working mothers and day nurseries. If only they had read *The House at Pooh Corner* with proper attention!

There they would find Kanga exemplifying Bowlby's 'it is an excellent plan to accustom babies and small children to being cared for now and then by someone else'.

In this instance, perhaps she also feels Roo should have some masculine company to balance his exclusively feminine society at home. This is admittedly speculative but it seems inherently probable.

## Roo's adventurous courage

Once again, Roo delights in experiences that would terrify a timid young creature and might worry even a comparatively bold one. When Tigger boasts he can climb trees better than Pooh, Roo is delighted to accept the invitation to ascend the tree on Tigger's back. When a bough breaks, nearly sending both of them to the ground, Roo said 'hopefully: "That was a lovely bit just now, when you pretended we were going to fall-bump-to-the-bottom, and we didn't. Will you do that bit again?"' So the only things Roo is not quite happy about are Tigger's refusal to repeat the 'pretend' fall and his refusal to climb to the very top of the tree.

## Pooh's innovative therapeutic technique in the tree incident

Some readers may object that Kanga was gravely mistaken in trusting her little son to the friendly but imprudent Tigger. However admirable Tigger's energy and Roo's pluck, the result was to leave them both treed. This criticism has some superficial plausibility, but superficial plausibility is precisely the sort of thing that the true Ursinologist distrusts. Probing deeper, as we always should, we see that here we have an excellent example of one of Pooh's innovative contributions to psychotherapeutic methodology: his use of patients' own freely chosen and totally independent activities as therapeutic techniques.

How does this work out in the incident we have just been examining? How does each of the participants in it benefit? Tigger learns the limits of his powers and the folly of boasting beyond them. Without losing his confidence or becoming pathologically suspicious, Roo has learnt not to take every claim at its face value. Piglet has learnt yet again not to take one of Pooh's obvious jokes literally and find dangerous 'jagulars' lurking on every branch. Christopher Robin, doubtless inspired by Pooh's own rescue of Piglet, finds an ingenious way of bringing Roo and Tigger safely to earth. Thus he justifies Kanga's earlier confidence in him, and builds up his own confidence in his ability to cope with the outer world which he must enter all too soon. Piglet's part is admittedly a minor one but it does foreshadow his major role in the rescue of Owl and Pooh. Eeyore manages to clothe his gloomy comments and prognostications with a not unpleasing sardonic wit. Pooh's own silence at the end of this episode fits in perfectly with his unobtrusive role in the whole incident.

We have not, unfortunately, any direct comment from Kanga, but we can scarcely doubt that she was pleased, even if slightly alarmed, by Roo's adventurous spirit. If she had been aware of Mary Ainsworth's work, she would have been gratified to find her success in giving her child a secure base acknowledged by the highest academic authority.

Nor can we doubt that she continues to regard Tigger with affectionate indulgence. Otherwise, we should not find him at Kanga's house, as a great friend of Roo. When he gets bored with waiting for the unbouncers, and goes home, Kanga greets him warmly with, 'There's a good Tigger. You're just in time for your Strengthening Medicine.'

> . . . then he and Roo pushed each other about in a friendly way, and Tigger accidentally knocked over one or two chairs by accident, and Roo accidentally knocked over one on purpose.

This relaxed play obviously enjoys Kanga's approval. We cannot imagine she would have tolerated an unwelcome visitor or unacceptable behaviour. Even when she seems to feel she has had enough of their mildly rowdy play, she utters no rebuke. She just diverts their energies by giving them a basket and telling them to go out and collect fir-cones for her.

As an exercise in cone collecting this was a failure. Roo and Tigger 'threw fir-cones at each other until they had forgotten what they came for, and they left the basket under the trees and went back to dinner.' Again there is no rebuke. We must, I think, conclude that Kanga's real purpose was simply to get them to let off steam out of the house. Another example of the close, though sometimes hidden, co-operation between Kanga and Pooh. The alert Ursinologist will see that Kanga was applying one of the latest techniques of modern psychotherapists. Many of them would recognize Tigger's 'bounciness' as typical of ADHT (Attention Deficiency Hyper Tension) syndrome. Many therapists today believe that active play is highly beneficial in such cases, and that insistence on quiet and stillness are futile and aggravate the trouble.

Just as Rabbit's failed attempt to 'unbounce' Tigger demonstrated his error, so Kanga's successful treatment demonstrated the correctness of her approach. And, of course, it shows her acting as, in some sense, Pooh's partner. So we Ursinologists may congratulate today's psychotherapists on catching up with Pooh and Kanga.

## Roo and Melanie Klein

Even Kanga cannot guarantee perfect happiness for Roo all the time. When Roo wants to join the expedition to unbounce Tigger, Kanga says:

> 'I think not to-day. Another day.'
> 'To-morrow?' said Roo hopefully.
> 'We'll see,' said Kanga.
> 'You're always seeing, and nothing ever happens,' said Roo sadly.

Later, when Christopher Robin and Tigger decide to go and find the missing unbouncers, Roo asks,

> 'May I find them too?' asked Roo eagerly.
> 'I think not to-day, dear,' said Kanga. 'Another day.'
> 'Well, if they're lost to-morrow, may I find them?'
> 'We'll see,' said Kanga. Roo . . . knew what *that* meant.

As so often in the Milnean texts, we find recognition of the darker side presented in the gentle way appropriate to the original audience. Thus we never find Roo expressing anger against Kanga, but we can hardly read those two dialogues without being reminded of Melanie Klein (1882–1960).

This unorthodox psychoanalyst agreed with the others we have been looking at in emphasizing the importance of play. She is perhaps even better known though for her distinction between the 'good' and the 'bad' mother. These were not two different kinds of mother, but the child's two different views of the same mother. These views were based entirely on the child's feelings at a particular moment. The mother was labelled 'good' when she gave what the child wanted; 'bad' when she thwarted these demands.

When Kanga thwarted Roo's desire to join his friends, he came as near to seeing her as a 'bad mother' as the whole context allowed.

## Roo and Piaget

Readers acquainted with developmental psychology must be waiting for some further reference to that eminent expert in the field, Jean Piaget (1896–1980). As some of them may have noticed already, there are many examples of Piagetian theory in the Milnean texts. Piaget recognized six stages of infancy. Young though Roo is, he has passed through and assimilated them. For example, when he plays Poohsticks, he clearly shows intentional activity (Piaget's Stage 3). At an earlier stage, an infant does not believe that an object exists if it is out of sight. So when Roo recognizes his own stick when it reappears, he understands that objects do continue to exist even when he cannot see them. This demonstrates he has reached Stage 4. Finally, when he looks for his stick on the side of the bridge opposite to that where he threw it in, he demonstrates he has reached Stage 6. At an earlier stage, he would have looked for the stick on the side where he last saw it, the wrong side.

Kanga conducted much of her highly successful bringing up of Roo on Piagetian lines. Piaget emphasized the *intellectual* importance of active play. This, he argued, helped to form mental structures vital in developing logical structures at a later stage. Thus, when Roo and Tigger threw fir cones at each other, Roo was laying the foundations for an understanding of ballistics.

Kanga is justified in being proud when Roo washes his face for the first time. We know from Piglet's uncomfortable experience that Kanga baths Roo every night. Familiarity with this process could have enabled Roo to imitate it mechanically by going through the motions of bathing someone or something else. But washing himself in a totally different environment – not a bath but the river — shows an understanding of the purpose of washing and the ability to apply it to himself.

When ascending the tree on Tigger's back, Roo says,

'That was a lovely bit just now, when you pretended we were going to fall-bump-to-the-bottom, and we didn't. Will you do that bit again?'

This goes beyond the earlier stage of merely repeating a pleasurable experience to the more advanced stage of remembering it (a mental act) and trying — though unsuccessfully in this case — to repeat it.

In passing, we should note that Piaget's picture of successive stages of mental development has often been seriously misunderstood. He found that these stages *usually* occurred at particular ages. He was far from saying that they must occur then. He emphasized 'Not the timing, but the order of succession.' Unfortunately, many teachers acquired an excessively rigid picture of the relation between age and stage of development. This sometimes led them actively to discourage exceptionally bright children whose mental development outstripped their chronological age.

Happily Kanga understood Piaget too well to hinder Roo's intellectual maturation. At the end of *The House at Pooh Corner*, Shepard's pictures show Roo had reached the stage of wanting to write. After examining his mother's and Tigger's signatures to the 'Rissolution', he tries to add his own, though he produces only 'SMUDGE'.

Milne skilfully avoided many problems by giving minimal information about dates and ages. This is particularly useful when considering Roo's development. He is articulate from the time we first meet him. His vocabulary is limited but not infantile. His syntax is correct with one interesting exception. When telling Tigger about his swim in the river, Roo says, 'I swimmed.' Though a mistake, it shows Roo was making linguistic progress. By adding '-ed' to the present tense of 'swim', he was applying the general rule for forming the past tense instead of merely parroting forms used by his elders (echolalia).

Roo enjoys new words. By the end of the Pooh saga, Roo shows linguistic creativity by inventing new words to fit new situations: describing Wol's bath-sponge (which Kanga had mistaken for a bunch of toadstools) as a 'spudge' ('sponge' plus sludge? or smudge?). We must not mistake Roo's originality for the common childish error of mispronouncing 'sponge' as 'spudge'. Milne reports Roo as saying clearly, 'It isn't a sponge, it's a spudge! Do you know what a spudge is, Owl?'

It is very obvious that Roo's verbal development goes side by side with his maturing in other respects. This strongly supports Margaret Donaldson's argument, clearly expressed in her *Children's Minds*, that children's language development is part of their general mental growth and does not need the once fashionable Chomskyan Language Acquisition Device.

It is natural, then, to find Roo's verbal sophistication paralleled by mental and psychological maturation. Piaget considered the very immature inevitably egocentric; not selfish in any culpable sense but psychologically incapable of recognizing any point of view except their own. Piaget calls the more mature ability to step outside of oneself 'decentring'. Roo demonstrates decentring when by his response when Kanga forbids him to join the search for Rabbit. He 'went into a corner and practised jumping out at himself, partly because he wanted to practise this, and partly because he didn't want Christopher Robin and Tigger to think he minded when they went off without him.' This shows an intelligent awareness of what others would probably think.

With even greater sophistication, Roo puts on an act to hide his real feelings. However dubious morally, the ability to dissimulate, even to lie, shows mental development, because it recognizes the independent reality of other minds, guesses intelligently what those minds are thinking, and controls the expression of one's own feelings in order to make the desired impression. Indeed, many modern psychologists, such as Uta Frith and Simon Baron-Cohen, think that *inability* to lie may reflect autism.

## Roo's moral development

This incident points out that an increase in maturity inevitably entails a loss of innocence and reveals the profoundly problematic nature of moral development. The account of Roo's moral development clearly implies a recognition of the two major schools of thought on this subject. One school regards morality as something learnt from others. The other school emphasizes the importance of the person's own moral growth. Pooh's eclectic approach leads us to expect that due importance will be paid to each school. This is precisely what we find. It is the combination of Kanga's influence as moral teacher and role model with Roo's own mental and moral growth that make him such a fine example of child development.

Throughout our account of Roo as a case study in childhood development and mother–child relations, we have been aware of Pooh as a benign influence. He has always seen that no one was hurt, either physically or psychologically. Yet he allowed his friends the freedom to work out and solve their own problems. In his respect for the individual person and his refusal to interfere unnecessarily, perhaps even more than in his wide and profound wisdom and professional expertise, Pooh Bear is an example to psychotherapists of every persuasion.

Piaget's influence on developmental and especially child psychology was deep and wide, but he was sometimes criticised for concentrating too exclusively on the individual and underestimating social influences. However it may be with Piaget, Pooh himself was well aware of and deeply concerned with social psychology. This has been amply and repeatedly demonstrated throughout this little introductory work. Even in this chapter, we have seen Roo learning to make friends with a wide variety of individuals and how to behave in the more formal society of a party.

## Case 6

### Wol's problems of communication

Readers may be surprised, even shocked, to find the learned Owl, or Wol as he writes his own name, presented as needing any kind of therapy. He is equally free from the hyperactivity of Tigger and the depression of Eeyore. Above all, he seems perfectly contented with his situation.

He does, however, have one recurrent problem: a difficulty in communication. Like many great scholars, he often finds it hard to express his wisdom and knowledge in language that the ordinary person can understand. It is here that Pooh's therapeutic skills come to his aid. Though Owl's problem may seem trivial compared with Pooh's other cases, it demanded all Pooh's tact as well as his psychological expertise. Like many scholars, Owl was somewhat touchy. If Pooh had told him bluntly that he should speak more plainly, Owl would probably have responded with indignation.

### Pooh's first visit to Owl

Pooh approaches Owl with a combination of genuine

respect with his assumed role of the Bear of Very Little Brain. Most Ursinologists will remember that Pooh had noticed that Eeyore had lost his tail and had promised to find it for him. His first step is to march to the Hundred Acre Wood, to consult Owl.

> 'And if anyone knows anything about anything,' said Bear to himself, 'it's Owl who knows something about something,' he said, 'or my name's not Winnie-the-Pooh,' he said. 'Which it is,' he added. 'So there you are.'

Arrived at The Chestnuts, Owl's 'old-world residence of great charm', Pooh inspects the notices at the entrance.

Underneath the knocker there was a notice which said:

PLES RING IF AN RNSER IS REQUIRD

Underneath the bell-pull there was a notice which said:

PLEZ CNOKE IF AN RNSR IS NOT REQUID

We need not here concern ourselves with the odd spelling in these notices. The text tells us plainly they had been written by Christopher Robin. We do notice the curious fact that the notice about ringing is placed under the knocker, while the notice about knocking is under the bell-pull. This is typical of the confusion that we often find in learned scholars when they have to deal with practical matters. This is particularly true when their approach is primarily verbal and abstract. Now nobody is more verbal and abstract than Owl. So these misplaced notices are a symptom of a general lack of awareness which is at the root of the problem that Pooh has to solve.

First, however, he is concerned with the problem of Eeyore's missing tail. After stating the problem, he asks Owl, 'So could you very kindly tell me how to find it for him?'

> 'Well,' said Owl, 'the customary procedure in such cases is as follows.'
>
> 'What does Crustimoney Proseedcake mean?' said Pooh. 'For I am a Bear of Very Little Brain, and long words Bother me.'
>
> 'It means the Thing to Do.'
>
> 'As long as it means that, I don't mind,' said Pooh humbly.
>
> 'The thing to do is as follows. First, Issue a Reward. Then — '

Once again, Pooh insists on simplification. Finally, Owl

134

says, 'We write a notice to say that we will give a large something to anybody who finds Eeyore's tail.'

In passing, we must pause to admire the skill with which Milne combines the storyline of the search for Eeyore's tail with the first stage of Pooh's work on improving Owl's communication skills. Everything in this dialogue bears on the quest for the missing tail. Yet at the same time it shows Pooh teaching Owl how to speak more simply. He does this without offending Owl. He allows him to keep his scholarly superiority and feel that he is kindly condescending to the limited capacity of the Bear of Very Little Brain.

It would be unrealistic to expect Owl to change the habits of a lifetime after just one brief therapeutic session. By now, I hope my readers know that profound realism underlies the surface fantasy of the Pooh saga. So it is no surprise to read that Owl immediately relapses. 'Owl went on and on, using longer and longer words, until at last he came back to where he started . . .' Pooh half dozes, answering 'Yes' and 'No' alternately, until he answers, 'No, not at all,' when Owl asks Pooh if he had seen the notices on Owl's front door.

This small section is packed with information relevant to Owl's problems. First we must enquire why Pooh was not listening to Owl. Second, what happened after Owl's surprise reawakened Pooh's attention. Most important of all, how do these questions link up with Pooh's treatment of Owl?

## Communication, awareness and social skills

The most obvious reason for Pooh's sleepy inattention was

135

boredom. Nothing is more boring than to hear someone talking at great length and using longer and longer words without saying anything of interest or importance. As a therapist, he had heard quite enough to realize he had a long haul ahead. It is even possible that he was relaxing to gather strength for his task.

There is, however, another reason. When Owl recommended offering 'a large something' to the finder of Eeyore's tail, this reminded Pooh that he usually had a 'small something' about that time of the morning. He reinforced this hint by looking wistfully at Owl's cupboard and murmuring, 'just a mouthful of condensed milk or what-not, with perhaps a lick of honey —' Owl totally ignores these clear hints and goes on talking.

How do we explain Owl's behaviour? We find few examples of his going out socially, but he is clearly prepared to receive visitors. The notices outside his door are proof positive of this. And he greets Pooh in a friendly way. Though a recluse then, he is certainly not inhospitable. We must look further for an explanation. Fortunately, we have not far to look. Those familiar with work of Michael Argyle will supply an answer. For all his good will, Owl lacks social skills.

Argyle has published many books about social skills; some written for academics, others for the general public. This ability to adapt language to circumstances is, as we have just seen, one of the main skills Pooh has to teach Owl. We have also noticed Owl's failure to respond appropriately to Pooh's body language. Body language is extremely important in all social situations. And here Shepard's illustration are specially illuminating.

The first picture of Owl and Pooh together might easily be misinterpreted. Owl's knitted brows might be read as showing anger because Pooh is unmistakably nodding off. A closer look reveals he is not looking at Pooh at all. His frown is a sign of his intense concentration on the lecture he is delivering. The illustration emphasizes Owl tendency to lecture rather than converse. And even lecturers, of course, should be aware of their audience, though all too many are not. On the previous page, Owl has taken Pooh out to show him the notices. Here he is beaming with the pride of ownership.

Social skills are often lacking in recluse scholars like Owl. They are, of course, closely bound up with communication and with general awareness of what is going on around. If Owl had been more aware of Pooh's body language, he would have noticed the wistful look

Pooh gave in the direction of Owl's cupboard. He would have realized that the Bear's remarks about his usual 'small something' were not mere items of information but a politely phrased request for refreshment. And he would have understood why Pooh gave 'a deep sigh' when his hints were disregarded.

Having finally roused Pooh's attention, Owl takes him outside to look at the notices, the knocker and the bell-rope. We know that Pooh had read notices very carefully when he arrived. We know too that he had used both knocker and bell-pull. But, concentrating on their function he had not closely observed these instruments. Now he did. And he recognized the bell-pull as Eeyore's missing tail.

Owl's account of how he had acquired it is further strong evidence of his unawareness of what was going on around him. His detachment from the trivia of everyday living are further evidenced when Pooh, having explained the facts, simply unhooked the tail and carried it back to Eeyore. Owl apparently accepts the loss of his bell-pull without comment.

Such detachment was convenient in this particular situation, but it must have brought home to Pooh that imparting all the varied aspects of social skills to Owl would be no easy task. There were, however, more urgent cases demanding his immediate attention. This, no doubt, is why Owl's progress seems to have been erratic, as evidenced when we meet him next, on the 'Expotition to the North Pole'.

## *Owl on the Expotition to the North Pole*

His first utterances on that occasion were admirably short, indeed monosyllabic: 'Come on!' and 'Hush!' From the point of view of social skills, they might be criticized as unnecessary and even officious. The same criticism might apply to his rather patronizing interruption of Pooh's whispered question. 'My dear Pooh,' said Owl in his superior way, 'don't you know what an ambush is?' The usually deferential Piglet is so indignant at this interruption that he protests:

> 'Owl,' said Piglet, looking round at him severely, 'Pooh's whisper was a perfectly private whisper, and there was no need —'

Undeterred by this rebuke, Owl goes on to explain that an ambush 'is a sort of surprise' and is 'when people jump out at you suddenly'. We must admit that his social skills are still insufficient to restrain his scholarly urge to impart information, even in unsuitable situations. He does, however, give the information in plain language and in simply constructed sentences. Pooh's influence is making itself felt. Almost immediately, though, there is a partial relapse. When Roo falls into the river:

> Owl was explaining that in a case of Sudden and Temporary Immersion the Important Thing was to keep the Head Above Water . . .

The key words 'keep the head above water' are simple enough, but their impact is weakened by the introductory phrase. Reference to a case makes it all abstract and impersonal, while 'Sudden and Temporary Immersion' still further removes the sense of urgency. Paradoxically, it may be the very feeling of crisis that startles Owl out of his newly acquired clarity and drives him back into his accustomed polysyllabics.

On the Expotition, he appears only once more, but then it in a particularly important situation. Right at the end, Christopher Robin has put up a notice recording Winnie-the-Pooh's discovery of the North Pole. Owl is at the back of the applauding crowd. His wings are outspread in what must be the nearest he can get to clapping. It is pleasant to see that he can appreciate a scientific discovery in a subject quite different from his own.

## Owl's progress

Owl next appears during the great flood that maroons Piglet. We remember that when Piglet was considering how his friends might deal with the situation, he remarks that Owl could escape by flying. It is highly significant to observe that, when Owl does appear, he is indeed flying, but not to escape the water. The text explicitly tells us '. . . Owl came flying over the water to say, "How do you do?" to his friend Christopher Robin.' This confirms our belief that Owl, despite his habitual reclusiveness, has his sociable side.

We learn from this short paragraph that he regards Christopher Robin as his friend, and that, undeterred by the weather, he makes a special visit to him. In the following conversation, Owl supplies evidence to both sides; to those who think Pooh has succeeded in radically simplifying Owl's language, and, on the other hand to those who stress his continued use of long words for simple things. On balance, surely we must agree that Owl has made vital progress. While he begins by making every statement first in his natural elaborate style, he proceeds to paraphrase in simpler language. So 'The atmospheric conditions have been very unfavourable lately,' becomes 'It has been raining.'

It is important to notice what triggers this series of simplifications. In every case it is a question that indicates that Christopher Robin has not understood Owl's original statement. That is to say that when Owl becomes aware of his hearer's limitations he alters his language accordingly. This advance in choosing appropriate language is also an advance in social skills.

Owl's last appearance during the flood makes a somewhat mixed impression. While Piglet is waiting for his rescuers, 'Owl . . . sat on a branch of his tree to comfort him, and told him a very long story about an aunt who had once laid a seagull's egg by mistake . . . ' We cannot doubt his good intentions: he sits on the branch to *comfort* Piglet (my emphasis). Obviously he hopes his story will distract Piglet from his fears. The actual result, however, is to endanger Piglet by sending him to sleep when he is hanging out of the window. We must remember, though, that Piglet is probably in an extremely unreceptive state. His mind is too full of a mixture of hope and anxiety to listen to even the most entertaining stories. Owl, as we shall see again, is overinclined to think that anecdotes about his relatives are necessarily interesting to other people. But he is at least trying to find topics of human interest rather than remote erudition. Moreover, so far as we can tell, he is using quite simple language.

## Owl and the party for Pooh

In a work as tightly structured as *Winnie-the-Pooh*, we must attach great importance to Owl's next appearance, towards the end of that volume. It is in a specifically social context. Christopher Robin summons Owl with a special whistle, and tells him he is giving a party in honour of Pooh's rescue of Piglet from the flood. He asks Owl to fly round and inform Pooh and invite all the others to the party. Whatever Christopher Robin's intellectual limitations may be, there is no doubt about his social skills. His choice of Owl as his messenger to the other guests is incontrovertible proof of Owl's visible improvement both in communication and social skills.

This improvement is also implied in a sentence at the end of his conversation with Christopher Robin, a sentence all too easily misinterpreted: 'Owl tried to think of something very wise to say, but couldn't, so he flew off to tell the others.' This is one of those occasions when I am tempted to despair of human intelligence: when the delight of reading and rereading the Milnean texts is temporarily shattered by the evidence of the gross misreadings to which those texts have been subjected.

Can my present readers believe that some people who claim to be true Pooh lovers take the sentence I have quoted in a negative sense. They suggest that Owl looked for pompous profundity, failed to find it, and therefore flew off. In truth, of course, he realized that when there was nothing important he could say, he had better say nothing. What an advance on that earlier appearance, when he had bored the tolerant Pooh Bear almost beyond endurance!

Owl continues his social progress when the party actually takes place. When Roo, who is at his very first party, says 'Hallo, Owl!' Owl says, '"Hallo, my little fellow," in a *kindly* way' (my italics). Owl then goes on 'telling Christopher Robin about an accident which had nearly happened to a friend of his whom Christopher Robin didn't know.' Not perhaps the most riveting conversation, but it does show he was aware that one should make conversation at a party.

## *Ups and downs of Owl's progress*

When we next meet Owl, it is during 'The Search for Small', early in *The House at Pooh Corner*. Shepard's picture clearly tells us that Owl is conducting an aerial reconnaissance as his contribution to the search. Moreover, Rabbit, who, naturally, is 'organdizing' the search, asks Pooh to meet him at Owl's house after he has looked for Small. Taken together, these facts make it clear that Owl is co-operating actively in this special kind of Neighbourhood Watch Scheme.

One weakness common to those with a special reputation for knowledge is a reluctance to admit ignorance. Sometimes – alas! – scholarly vanity gets the better of scholarly accuracy. Owl shows this weakness when Rabbit asks him to explain the strange messages he had found on or fallen from Christopher Robin's door. At first he interprets

GON OUT

BACKSON

BISY

BACKSON

C.R.

quite reasonably as meaning that Christopher Robin has gone out with Backson and that they are busy together. But then he seems to think that a Backson is a specific kind of creature. When Rabbit asks what Backsons are like, Owl flounders before admitting frankly, 'I don't know *what* they're like.'

## Owl displays true social skills

It is pleasing to record that his next appearance shows him at his best. Pooh and Piglet are going to have 'a Proper Tea with Owl'. On the way they have a word with Eeyore. He tells them that Owl had flown past a day or two ago 'and noticed me. He didn't actually say anything, mind you, but he knew it was me. Very friendly of him, I thought. Encouraging.' This little incident may not seem to show much social skill on Owl's part, but we must interpret it in the light of Eeyore's way of looking at things and reporting them. The essential thing is that Eeyore was pleased at what he explicitly saw as a sign of friendship.

Whatever doubts we may have about this, there can be none about the implications of the statement that they were going to have a Proper Tea with Owl. This would be meaningless unless they had good reason to expect a satisfying tea at The Chestnuts. Such expectation must be founded on one of two things: either a definite invitation to tea or previous experiences of good teas when they had dropped in casually.

We are not left in doubt for long. The opening conversation makes it clear they were hopeful droppers-in rather than invited guests. When they arrive, ' "Hallo, Owl," said Pooh. "I hope we're not too late for — I mean, how are you, Owl? Piglet and I just came to see how you were because it's Thursday." ' He courteously checks himself from any explicit reference to tea. Owl greets his guests warmly and they settle down to discuss that traditional topic of English social chat, the weather.

Owl's part in the conversation now combines clarity with a certain scholarly flavour. He has now found a happy medium between excessive erudition and, to him, untypical brevity. Pooh's lesson in communication has now been truly assimilated. True, 'blusterous' is an unusual form of the word. In the context of the gale outside, however, no one could doubt its meaning.

When the gale turns Owl's house on its side, the plates and cups and saucers now scattered on the floor in Shepard's picture strongly suggest that Owl's table had been set for several people. Thus Pooh's expectations are confirmed, though their gratification is postponed.

Owl is naturally startled by this violent disruption of his charming old-world residence. He is so much shaken out of his normal rationality that at first he suspects that Pooh was responsible. When Piglet corrects this absurd error, Owl quickly regains his grasp of reality. When Piglet asks how they can get out now that storm damage has blocked the door, Owl replies, 'That is the Problem, Piglet, to which I am asking Pooh to give his mind.'

His confidence is soon rewarded. Pooh announces a plan that fully deserves Owl's praise of him as an 'Astute and Helpful Bear'. This is certainly the most accurate estimate of Winnie-the-Pooh that is uttered by any character in the whole Pooh saga. It is supremely appropriate that it is Owl who pronounces it. It fully justifies his own reputation as one who knows things.

The wisdom of Pooh's plan and Piglet's courage in executing have been detailed in the chapter on Piglet. All we need add to this remarkable incident is the restored serenity with which Owl settles down to entertain Pooh, his remaining guest, by finishing the story about his Uncle Robert, which had been interrupted by the collapse of Owl's tree home. Once again we notice his pleasure in telling stories about his relatives.

## *The other Forest dwellers join to help Owl*

If anyone has ever doubted the high regard the other Forest dwellers had for the learned Owl, those doubts must vanish when they read that everybody but Eeyore was there helping to get Owl's belongings 'out of his old house so as to be ready to put them into his new one'. As we shall see in a moment, Eeyore has his own part to play. Meanwhile Owl's own words show both the domestic confusion traditionally associated with scholarly bachelors and their rather irritated defence of their own life-style.

When Kanga, doubtless an immaculate housewife, suggests he wouldn't want an old dish-cloth and a carpet full of holes, 'Owl was calling back indignantly, "Of course I do! It's just a question of arranging the furniture properly, and it isn't a dishcloth, it's my shawl." '

Kanga gets a little flustered because she couldn't keep an eye on Roo all the time.

> So she got cross with Owl and said that his house was a Disgrace, all damp and dirty, and it was quite time it did tumble down. Look at that horrid bunch of toadstools growing out of the corner there? So Owl looked down, a little surprised because he didn't know about this, and then gave a short sarcastic laugh, and explained that this was his sponge.

This little irritation is perfectly understandable during a house move, notoriously a major source of stress.

Fortunately it is soon dispelled, first by Roo's delightful description of Owl's sponge as a spudge, then by Pooh's new song about Piglet's heroic rescue of Pooh and Owl. Owl then displays the name-board of his new house: THE WOLERY. As Christopher Robin says, 'so now all he wants is the house.'

This problem is solved when the deus ex machina appears in the rather surprising form of Eeyore. Eeyore announces that he has found the required house and proposes to show it to Christopher Robin. It is well worth noticing Owl's behaviour. When Rabbit urges Owl to follow Eeyore and Christopher Robin, ' "Wait a moment," said Owl, picking up his notice-board . . .'

Even at this exciting moment, a moment which concerns him closely, he maintains his scholarly regard for the written word. When he looks at the board more closely, he is naturally displeased to find his new address had become THE SMEAR. He 'coughed at Eeyore sternly', for it was Eeyore who had changed THE WOLERY to THE SMEAR by sitting on the notice before it had dried. In the past, Owl might have rebuked Eeyore severely. Now, however, he realizes that it would be unkind and inappropriate to hurt Eeyore's feelings when he was performing a major act of kindness to Owl. So he remains silent.

Pooh must have been delighted by this proof of his success in improving Owl's social skills.

Many readers have noticed that this is Owl's last personal appearance. Perhaps we should take it for granted

that he would follow to see his new house. But the text
does not explicitly say so. Arrived at the house, Eeyore and
Piglet agree that it's 'just the house for Owl'. In this
situation, we should expect to find some comment from
Owl himself. Again, both Eeyore and Piglet speak of him
in the third person. In the whole of this scene, nobody
addresses him directly.

How can we explain this? Is Owl so offended by the
damage to his sign that he refuses to join the party? This
would imply a sulky reaction wholly at variance with his
character. It would also imply that Pooh's therapy has
failed catastrophically, which is unthinkable. Does he
simply consider Eeyore is highly unlikely to be a good
house finder? This is quite conceivable. Indeed, his
scepticism proves justified when we learn that the house
Eeyore has found for Owl is Piglet's. Nevertheless, to
ignore Eeyore's suggestion completely would still show
Owl behaving in a distinctly ungracious manner. We need
to search further.

The vitality of all the Pooh characters is so convincing
that we sometimes forget that everything we know about
them comes from the recorded texts. We must remember too
that the recorder was a master of narrative art. An essential
element of this art lies in knowing how to focus the reader's
attention on whatever is most important at any given
moment. This obviously entails omitting material – however
fascinating in itself – that might distract us from that.

Now what was overwhelmingly important at this
moment? Two things: Piglet's noble gesture in sacrificing

his own much loved house to Owl, and his supreme reward when Christopher Robin asks Piglet, 'What would you do, if your house was blown down?' and Pooh answers for him: 'He'd come and live with me, wouldn't you, Piglet?'

At this supreme moment in Piglet's life, even Owl's move must take a back seat. No longer puzzled by Owl's apparent absence, we can recognize yet another example of Milne's masterly skill. He has already told us in the heading to this chapter that Owl did in fact move into the Wolery that Eeyore had found. He has told us all we need to know and refrained from distracting us with unnecessary information. In a chapter largely concerned with Owl, I find this silence alludes obliquely to Owl's progress. I hope no one will suspect me of being over-subtle or far-fetched when I suggest that the silences we have been considering *enact* the progress that Owl has made.

The once verbose Owl has learnt to go straight to the point. He has also learnt when polysyllables are appropriate and when the simplest vocabulary is required. He now exercises the social skills of hospitality and tactful silence. Another triumph for Winnie-the-Pooh, super-therapist.

## Case 7

### Eeyore: a case of clinical depression

#### Eeyore's transformation

We first meet Eeyore in his Gloomy Place, solitary, thinking sadly, and answering Pooh's "And how are you?" with 'Not very how. I don't seem to have felt at all how for a long time.'

Yet at the end of the Pooh saga, it is Eeyore who proposes a 'Rissolution' to the departing Christopher Robin, and reads out a poem of his own composition. What has caused this remarkable transformation from loneliness and depression to taking centre stage and the leading position at such an important moment in the life of the Forest?

#### Varied lights on Eeyore

The beginning of psychology as an independent science is usually dated from 1879, when a psychological laboratory was founded by Wilhelm Wundt (1832–1920). He and his American student, Edward Titchener laid down a method of carefully trained introspection. This would analyse our minds into a vast number – more than 46,708 according to Titchener – of elementary sensations. In contrast, in the first half of the twentieth century, the leaders of Gestalt psychology. Max Wertheimer, Wolfgang Kohler and Kurt Koffka, argued that, in reality, we perceive, not elements but wholes, wholes that form patterns. Eeyore was unmistakably referring to this in Chapter Five of *The House at Pooh Corner*.

> Eeyore had laid three sticks on the ground . . . Two of the sticks were touching at one end, but not at the other, and the third stick was laid across *them*.

Eeyore explains that to most people – perhaps referring to the Wundt–Titchener school – 'It's just three sticks to them. But to the educated . . . it's a great and glorious 'A'.'

If any sceptic doubts the reference, their doubts will be dispelled when they remember that Gestalt psychologists dismiss the concept that elementary sensations are tied together 'like a *bundle of sticks*' (my emphasis). Could the connection be plainer?

Kurt Lewin (1890–1947) was early influenced by the Gestalt school but developed an approach of his own. In one passage, he describes how exactly the same scene would appear quite different to a holiday-maker taking a country stroll and to a soldier during a battle. Remembering this, should we interpret Eeyore's 'gloomy place' as a reflection of his mood rather than as an objective descriptive?

This is tempting but I think we should resist the temptation, as indeed we should always be on our guard against far-fetched connections. The last thing I want to recommend to my fellow students are superficially attractive but fundamentally unsound solutions. In this case, there is too much evidence from unimpeachable sources that Eeyore's dwelling was truly a gloomy place.

Once again I would call my readers' attention to the end-paper map to *Winnie-the-Pooh*. There, in the bottom right-hand corner, we find, not only the unequivocal label 'Eeyore's Gloomy Place', but the additional and clinching words 'Rather Boggy and *Sad*' (my emphasis).

We must, I think, conclude that, though Gestalt concepts illuminate some aspects of Eeyore's psyche, we have to look elsewhere for an explanation of his radical change of mood. I hope to show, beyond all reasonable doubt, that this explanation lies in the comparatively new school of Cognitive Psychology.

By this time, no psychologically instructed Ursinologist can hesitate in giving the credit to Winnie-the-Pooh himself. Such an Ursinologist is indisputably correct, but may still be wondering how our great therapist effected this almost miraculous cure. It is now our pleasing task to answer this question.

## How Pooh used Cognitive Psychology to cure Eeyore's depression

*Chambers 21st Century Dictionary* defines 'cognition' as 'knowing in the widest sense, including sensation, perception, etc.'. Cognitive Psychology argues that many psychological disorders are caused by false knowledge and distorted perception. These are a particularly common source of depression. So it was very natural that Winnie-the-Pooh should choose this form of therapy to cure the depression that was Eeyore's usual state at the beginning of the Pooh saga.

Eeyore first appears standing 'by himself in a thistly part of the Forest'. Immediately after, we read:

Sometimes he thought sadly to himself, 'Why?' and sometimes he thought, 'Wherefore?' and sometimes he thought, 'Inasmuch as which?' – and sometimes he didn't quite know what he was thinking about.

As we have learnt to expect from our author, this introductory passage is full of vital information. Right away, we see that he was solitary and that he was in a thistly part of the Forest. At this stage, we do not know why he was solitary. We shall discover in due course.

Then we read he was thinking 'sadly'. And these sad thoughts were all questions. He does not even consider any answers. Now, to have one's mind full of nothing but unanswered questions is itself a deeply depressing situation. When we examine Eeyore's questions, we see that they are so vaguely worded that no answers are possible.

In other words, Eeyore is depressing himself by a false perception of the true nature of questions. His failure to do the impossible drives him to mental confusion described in the sentence quoted from the text. No wonder he was very glad when Winnie-the-Pooh arrived and interrupted these gloomy thoughts.

Even then, he greeted Pooh in such a gloomy manner

that the great – and always sympathetic – therapist realized at once that help was needed. His 'How are you?' was not primarily the conventional formula of greeting but his therapist's enquiry into a patient's state.

Pooh's investigation brings to his notice the fact that Eeyore's tail is missing.

> 'That Accounts for a Good Deal,' said Eeyore gloomily. 'It Explains Everything. No Wonder.'
> 'You must have left it somewhere,' said Winnie-the Pooh.
>    'Somebody must have taken it,' said Eeyore. 'How Like Them.'

We notice how Eeyore jumps immediately from the comparatively rational opinion that the loss of his tail accounts for a good deal to the obvious exaggeration that it explains everything. Cognitive psychologists describe such errors of perception as mental filters (filtering out all but one fact, usually an unpleasant one) magnification (exaggerating, for example, the importance of the tail. After all, he had not even noticed its disappearance until Pooh pointed it out to him).

Then he accuses someone of having taken it. This turns out to be correct but he goes to say this is typical of 'Them'. Assuming that 'They' habitually act harmfully is a characteristic example of what Cognitive Psychologists call 'Overgeneralization'. So here we have a cluster of distortions. How does Pooh respond? 'Pooh felt that he ought to say something helpful about it, but didn't quite know what. So he decided to do something helpful instead.' He announces that he will find the missing tail.

At this stage, some therapists may question Pooh's judgement. Surely, they may say, Pooh should have built up Eeyore's self-esteem by persuading him to find the missing tail himself, rather than relying on his therapist.

In previous Ursinological studies, I have shown that if ever we feel tempted to attribute error to Winnie-the-Pooh, more thought will show us the error is never in him but always in ourselves. The rightness of his judgement here is shown doubly. Look at Eeyore's immediate response: 'Thank you, Pooh. You're a real friend. Not Like Some.' That is, Pooh has persuaded Eeyore that he is not totally alone. He has at least one friend. We see later that his conviction that he is friendless is a major cause of his depression. Pooh has brought him to take the first step in correcting this serious cognitive distortion.

Secondly, when Pooh has recovered the tail – quite unwittingly taken by Wol – and Christopher Robin has nailed it back in its proper place, 'Eeyore frisked about the forest, waving his tail so happily that Winnie-the-Pooh came over all funny, and had to hurry home for a little snack of something to sustain him.'

There are two significant facts for us to note that the end of this stage in Eeyore's transformation. (a) By co-opting Christopher Robin, Pooh demonstrates that Eeyore has another friend. (b) Pooh's own pleasure and pride in this success shows us that his expertise does not exclude warm feeling, though his professionalism reserves expressing this until he is in private.

## A difficult case for Pooh Bear

At this stage, some readers who are more familiar with the Milnean texts than with psychotherapy may raise an objection. It is all very well, they may say, to leave Eeyore frisking about, as happy as can be. But when we meet him next, he has relapsed into the deepest gloom.

> Eeyore, the old grey Donkey, stood by the side of the stream, and looked at himself in the water.
> 'Pathetic,' he said. 'That's what it is. Pathetic.'
> Then, looking at his reflection from the other side –
> 'As I thought,' he said. 'No better from *this* side. But nobody minds. Nobody cares. Pathetic, that's what it is.'

Such doubters will probably add that Eeyore has not only returned to his early depression but also to the cognitive distortion that lies at its base. Totally forgetting the caring help he received from Pooh and Christopher Robin, he still says that nobody cares.

Far from being evidence that Pooh has failed, this episode is clear proof of the solid realism of the whole Pooh opus, a realism which I have humbly tried to imitate in my Ursinological studies. In general, psychotherapists agree that long-standing psychological problems cannot be truly solved in a single session.

Too often, clients expect their therapist to be a magician who can cure all their ills with the wave of a magic wand. One consultant was actually told this in so many words. Others are less explicit but clearly cherish the same illusory hope. With his accustomed realism, Winnie-the-Pooh recognizes that Eeyore has been building his depressive state over a long time. It has become a settled habit. The Cognitive approach does not demand the months, even years, that the analytical schools often require, but it does take a little time. Let us see then how Pooh Bear continues when he finds Eeyore in the state just described.

First, no doubt, he notices Eeyore's body language. Shepard's illustration brings this emphatically to our notice. Even if the text had not just told us that Eeyore is gazing *gloomily* (my emphasis) at his own reflection, his posture clearly signifies dejection. Moreover, it prevents him from seeing the always cheerful sight of a dragonfly. Eeyore's gloomy response to Pooh's greeting confirms the overall picture of depression.

When Pooh asks Eeyore what is the matter with him –

'Nothing, Pooh Bear, nothing. We can't all, and some of us don't. That's all there is to it.'

'Can't all what?' said Pooh, rubbing his nose.

'Gaiety. Song-and-dance. Here we go round the mulberry bush.'

'Oh!' said Pooh. He thought for a long time, and then asked, 'What mulberry bush is that?'

I must break off at this moment , to correct – yet again – a recurrent error. Incredible as it may seem after the varied Ursinological studies of recent years, there are still some who may interpret Pooh's question as a sign of incomprehension, even of stupidity. This, of course, springs from the fundamental error of taking the description of Pooh as 'a Bear of Very Little Brain' at its face value. In face of the massive evidence to the contrary, this must itself be categorized as an example of cognitive distortion. Whether they know it or not, correcting this distortion is what all Ursinologists are engaged in doing.

Pooh's question is an attempt to bring Eeyore from metaphor to fact, from fantasy to reality. Eeyore's reply 'Bon-hommy . . .' shows that Pooh's first attempt has failed. No wonder he 'sat down on a large stone, and tried to think this out'.

After my recent warning, all my readers should be on their guard against a literal interpretation of 'It sounded like a riddle, and he was never much good at riddles, being a Bear of Very Little Brain. So he sang *Cottleston Pie* instead.' Anyone who reads this song attentively must see that it does in fact describe some of the fundamental principles of Cognitive Psychology.

The second line goes, 'A fly can't bird, but a bird can fly.' That is, the first half denies the cognitively distorted idea that a fly could bird, while the second half states the positive, cognitively correct statement that a bird can fly. The corresponding line in the second verse, 'A fish can't whistle and neither can I', dismisses two more errors. The second line of the third verse poses a slightly different problem: 'Why does a chicken, I don't know why.' As the apparent question is, as stated, meaningless, there is no meaningful answer. By accepting this, Pooh avoids the trap of setting himself an impossible task.

This trap is particularly tempting to exceptionally able people who set themselves unrealistically high standards. Frederick Perls followed Pooh by warning us against perfectionism, and it has been regarded as a major cause of cognitive distortion. Those who fall into this trap make themselves miserable by continually underrating their real achievements because not everything they do reaches perfection.

Avoiding both the Scylla of misperception and the Charybdis of perfectionism, Pooh Bear reminds himself of the basic principles of the particular psychology he is applying to Eeyore. He continues calmly with his therapeutic task. This alone should convince us that anyone who thinks that Pooh really is a Bear of Very Little Brain is making the error of 'labelling'.

Questioning further, Pooh discovers that Eeyore is particularly sad just then because it is his birthday and nobody has remembered it: '. . . no presents and no cake and no candles, and no proper notice taken of me at all'. At first sight, Eeyore seems to have a good reason for his unhappiness. We should all feel unhappy at having our birthday ignored. In fact, though, nobody knew it was his birthday. Pooh was greatly surprised to hear it, and if he didn't know, we can take it nobody else knew either.

This is not an uncommon situation with depressives. As well as dreaming up imaginary causes of unhappiness, they often create sad situations which are real enough but are the result of their own action – or inaction. Knowing how friendly the Forest dwellers were, we can be sure they would have responded appropriately to Eeyore's birthday if they had known about it. Had he sent out any invitations? Had he told anybody? Obviously not.

Pooh was far too wise, as well as far too kind, to point this out just then. That would merely have exacerbated Eeyore's already gloomy state of mind. Instead, he took immediate action to show Eeyore — again — that he was not without friends who cared for his happiness. First he fetches a pot of his precious honey. Then he congratulates Piglet on deciding to give Eeyore a balloon: 'That, Piglet, is a very good idea. It is just what Eeyore wants to cheer him up. Nobody can be uncheared with a balloon.' Owl contributes an impressively long inscription for the pot: 'HIPY PAPY BTHUTHDTH THUTHDA BTHUTHDY'. This, he tells Pooh, actually says, 'A Very Happy Birthday with love from Pooh.'

In spite of the unplanned changes that befall both presents before they reach Eeyore, he ends up 'as happy as could be'. Right at the end, we read that the always kindly Christopher Robin had given him a box of paints, and had also arranged a party for him, with 'a cake with icing on the top, and three candles, and his name in pink sugar . . .'

Already Eeyore has made important progress, but he still has a long way to go.

Already, Pooh has corrected several of Eeyore's false perceptions. Eeyore now realizes that, despite his solitary habits, he has many friends, who have contributed to give him a truly HIPY BTHUTHDTH.

## *Eeyore takes a step forward.*

When we next Eeyore, he has joined the Expotition to the North Pole. His participation in a group activity is itself an enormous step forward. True he was a reluctant member – 'I didn't want to come on this Expo – what Pooh said. I only came to oblige.' The important fact is that he did come, however reluctantly and inclined to grumble.

Moreover, when Baby Roo falls into the river, Eeyore immediately springs to the rescue.

> Eeyore had turned round and hung his tail over the first pool into which Roo fell, and with his back to the accident was grumbling quietly to himself, and saying, 'All this washing . . . but catch on to my tail, little Roo, and you'll be all right.'

Unfortunately, owing to his habitual unawareness of what is actually happening, he took his stance upstream of where Roo had been swept to. However, though he gave no practical help, his active goodwill was beyond doubt. So was his perseverance, for, still unaware of what was happening, he remained at his station long after Roo had been rescued. And this despite his growing discomfort as his tail gets colder and colder.

Some readers may be puzzled that it was Christopher Robin who rubbed Eeyore's numb tail back to life, while Pooh seems ignorant of the situation, and even somewhat unsympathetic to Eeyore's plight. When Eeyore says, 'I

thought you were saying how sorry you were about my tail, being all numb, and could you do anything to help?' Pooh replies, 'No . . . That wasn't me . . . Perhaps it was somebody else.'

Pooh's attitude is perfectly clear when we remember that Christopher Robin had already dried Eeyore's tail. This had given him both the obvious material comfort and also another reminder that he had friends who genuinely cared for him. To ask for more, as Eeyore had just done, was to indulge in a combination of self-pity and an excessive demand for more sympathy. No good psychologist would pander to such unhealthy emotions. Pooh knew that there are occasions when a salutary neglect is the best way to induce the independence and self-reliance that is the true aim of every therapist.

Even in the short term, this produced an encouraging

result. Eeyore's last words in this chapter were: 'Well, anyhow – it didn't rain.' A very upbeat comment in the circumstances.

When the great flood leaves Piglet entirely surrounded by water, he thinks how his friends may be coping with the situation. When he comes to Eeyore, he says, 'And Eeyore is so miserable anyhow that he wouldn't mind about this.' We need hardly be surprised that Piglet is unaware of Eeyore's progress, but he does implicitly credit him with a certain Stoical armour against the slings and arrows of outrageous fortune. Perhaps it was this that gave Eeyore the inward strength on which Pooh was able to work with such spectacular success.

This success was still a good way off, as we see on the occasion of the party that Christopher Robin gave in honour of Pooh's rescue of Piglet. When Wol delivers the invitation to Eeyore, Eeyore refuses at first to believe it is meant for him. Initially he professes not to know what an invitation is. When Wol explains '. . . it's asking you to the party –

Eeyore shook his head slowly.

'You mean Piglet. The little fellow with the excited ears. That's Piglet. I'll tell him.'

'No, no!' said Owl, getting quite fussy. 'It's you!'

'Are you sure?'

'Of course I'm sure. Christopher Robin said 'All of them! Tell all of them.'

'All of them, except Eeyore?'

'All of them,' said Owl sulkily.

'Ah!' said Eeyore.

'A mistake, no doubt, but still, I shall come. Only don't blame me if it rains.'

When he does come, he surprisingly assumes that the party is for him. Extreme mood swings like are by no means uncommon in depressives. What is striking is that he starts to make quite a fluent, indeed impressive speech of thanks. Even when he is disillusioned, though disappointed, he does not break down or stalk off in dudgeon. Instead, he takes refuge in irony:

'After all, one can't complain. I have my friends. Somebody spoke to me only yesterday. And was it last week or the week before that Rabbit bumped into me and said 'Bother!' The Social Round. Always something going on.'

All too characteristically, he takes a sour grapes attitude to the Special Pencil Case presented to Pooh:

'This writing business. Pencils and what-not. Over-rated, if you ask me. Silly stuff. Nothing in it.'

At this stage, his attitude to education contrasts sharply with what we noticed earlier in discussing how his recognition of 'A' illustrated Gestalt Psychology.

Thus, at the end of *Winnie-the-Pooh*, Pooh's therapeutic work on Eeyore has still much to achieve. The first

Ursinologists must have felt a mixture of hope and impatience. Surely the great author would not leave this taxing case study unfinished. But how long would students have to wait? Two years, as we fortunate later scholars know. In *The House at Pooh Corner*, we find him completing his greatest therapeutic triumph.

Clearly aware of his public's eagerness to know how Eeyore's case was proceeding, Milne recorded the next stage in the very first chapter of his second volume. Even the most superficial reader will remember that this volume begins with Pooh's taking Piglet for a walk in the snow. As they near Eeyore's Gloomy Place, they sit on top of a gate, and sing Pooh's latest composition, his 'Good Hum, such as is Hummed Hopefully to Others'. When they have done this six times, Pooh says, 'I've been thinking about Eeyore.' He points out that Eeyore is the only one in the Forest who hasn't got a house. 'We will build it here,' said Pooh, just by this wood, out of the wind, because this is where I thought of it. And we will call this Pooh Corner. And we will build an Eeyore House with sticks at Pooh Corner for Eeyore.' Piglet has noticed a heap of sticks on the other side of the wood. So they set off to fetch the sticks and build a house for Eeyore.

Meanwhile, Eeyore has been telling Christopher Robin how cold he has been 'with all this snow and one thing and another, not to mention icicles and such-like'. It is worth commenting on that, even while reciting his song of sorrow, he does recognize that, when the others belatedly realize his sufferings, 'they'll be Sorry'. However tinged with self-pity Eeyore's remarks may be, Pooh's therapy has already brought him to recognize that the others would sympathize if they had Brains enough to understand.

Eeyore goes on to tell Christopher Robin that he had built a house for himself. This in itself shows a remarkable advance in active self-help. But –

'The really exciting part,' said Eeyore in his most melancholy voice, 'is that when I left it this morning it was there, and when I came back it wasn't. Not at all, very natural, and it was only Eeyore's house. But I still just wondered.'

When Eeyore and the kindly Christopher Robin arrive at the site of Eeyore's house, Pooh and Piglet are just finishing The Eeyore House at Pooh Corner. It soon becomes clear to everybody except Eeyore that the 'heap of sticks' used to build the house was in fact Eeyore's original house. Eeyore decides that

'the wind blew it right over the wood, and blew it down here, and here it is as good as ever. In fact, better in places.'

'Much better, said Pooh and Piglet together.

'It just shows what can be done by taking a little trouble,' said Eeyore. 'Do you see, Pooh? Do you see, Piglet? Brains first and then Hard Work. Look at it! *That's* the way to build a house,' said Eeyore proudly.

In this episode, Pooh combines practical, material assistance with a truly remarkable ability to seize a totally unexpected opportunity to fortify Eeyore's self-esteem. No wonder that we also find here a powerful signal from Milne himself. Serious Ursinologists are repeatedly amazed by the way in which many devoted lovers of Pooh fail to pick up the signals our author sends us. This is particularly astonishing in our present case. What does the very title refer to? Who was the House at Pooh Corner built for? Eeyore. What was its full original title? The *Eeyore* House at Pooh Corner (my emphasis). Pooh himself remains the only character whose name appears openly in either title; in fact, in both. But Eeyore has the secondary but unique honour of a submerged but easily detected reference to the title of the last volume of the Pooh opus.

## *Eeyore makes further advances in sociability*

Eeyore's response to the arrival of the Bouncy Tigger is extremely interesting. It is fundamentally hospitable but also somewhat clumsy. When Tigger has discovered that Tiggers don't like honey and haycorns but announces that 'Thistles is what Tiggers like best,' Pooh and Piglet take him to Eeyore's thistly habitat. After Pooh has introduced them, Piglet explains, 'He's just come.'

> 'Ah,' said Eeyore again.
> He thought for a long time and then said:
> 'When is he going?'

Though still lacking in social skills, Eeyore generously offers the stranger 'A little patch I was keeping for my birthday . . .' When Tigger discovers that Tiggers *don't* like thistles, Eeyore's only complaint is the eminently reasonable one: 'Then why bend a perfectly good one?' He also denies Piglet's comment – to Tigger – that Eeyore was *always* gloomy, saying that 'on the contrary, he was feeling particularly cheerful this morning'.

## *Eeyore helps to rescue Tigger and Roo*

When Pooh and Piglet were considering the situation of the treed Tigger and Roo, 'Christopher Robin and Eeyore came strolling along together'. This fact shows a marked improvement in Eeyore's sociability. We can imagine Pooh's pleasure. Pooh would also know that Christopher

Robin's cheerful temperament was the perfect counterbalance to the depressive traits that still lingered in Eeyore. Thus, when Eeyore makes his usual gloomy weather forecasts, 'Christopher Robin didn't much mind *what* it did tomorrow, as long as he was out in it.'

This ability to use others' qualities to assist his therapeutic task is, as we see again and again, one of Pooh's outstanding skills. It is closely allied to his modesty, a quality not universally found in eminent psychologists. He shows another example of this when he allows Christopher Robin to take the lead in the rescue of Roo and Tigger. We have often been pained to note Christopher Robin's blindness to the wisdom of the Great Bear. On the other hand, we have always acknowledged his courtesy, good will and practical skill. We can be sure that whatever we noticed, Pooh noticed. Tactfully, he guided his friend towards the practical career in which he was well qualified to shine.

Before Christopher Robin announces his plan, Piglet ventures his suggestion: "I thought," said Piglet earnestly, "that if Eeyore stood at the bottom of the tree, and if Pooh stood on Eeyore's back, and if I stood on Pooh's shoulders —"'

Though Eeyore objects, he does so with a pleasing black humour:

> 'And if Eeyore's back snapped suddenly, then we could all laugh. Ha ha! Amusing in a quiet way,' said Eeyore, 'but not really helpful.'

After the tunic plan has been announced, Eeyore condenses and clarifies the objectives of the exercise for Piglet's benefit: '*Getting Tigger down,*' said Eeyore, 'and *Not hurting anybody.* Keep those two ideas in your head, Piglet, and you'll be all right.' This little speech alone shows how far Eeyore has progressed in ridding himself of cognitive errors.

Even when Tigger's jump from the tree leaves Eeyore at the bottom of the heap, Eeyore does not utter a word of complaint, though we may detect a certain sarcasm when he asks Christopher Robin to thank the now safe and Bouncy Tigger for him.

## *Eeyore learns he has more friends than he had thought*

One of Eeyore's most harmful cognitive errors was his belief that nobody cared for him. Pooh realizes this will take repeated contrary evidence to uproot. And the repetition will be the more convincing the more different friends supply it. Pooh himself of course, Christopher Robin and Piglet. Now Piglet is to have another turn. This time his action is all the more impressive because he performs it by himself and entirely on his own initiative, though doubtless inspired by Pooh. Piglet has just picked himself a bunch of violets, when —

> ... it suddenly came over him that nobody had ever picked Eeyore a bunch of violets, and the more he thought of this, the more he thought how sad it was to be an Animal who never had a bunch of violets picked for him.

174

Piglet arrives with the violets when Eeyore is preoccupied with constructing a capital 'A' with three sticks. Because he is thus engaged, he hardly notices Piglet's kindly offering. Then he is angry to find that, far from being restricted to a small elite, 'A' is a thing that even Rabbit knows. We may learn several important lessons from this episode.

First, although Eeyore ignores Piglet's violets, Piglet stands firm and finally leaves the flowers for Eeyore to enjoy in a more suitable mood. While Pooh's major success in developing Piglet's independence is the subject of Case 3, we can hardly ignore this example of it.

Secondly, Eeyore's ungracious reception of Piglet's charming present reminds us that his social skills were still unreliable. We must hope that when Eeyore had recovered his equilibrium, he noticed, appreciated and acknowledged Piglet's generosity.

## The turning point for Eeyore

We have already seen that Pooh's use of Cognitive Therapy has made a considerable improvement in Eeyore, but the turning point comes in Chapter Six of *The House at Pooh Corner*, a chapter entitled, most significantly, 'In which Pooh invents a new game and *Eeyore joins* in' (my emphasis).

Nowhere does our text combine literary skill with psychological realism better than in Eeyore's next appearance and its consequences. Outside the text itself, perhaps few things have given greater pleasure than the game of Poohsticks. 'Now one day Pooh and Piglet and Rabbit and Roo were all playing Poohsticks together.' Piglet is very excited because he thinks his stick – a big grey one – is winning. But the big grey stick turns out to be Eeyore.

Though he tells his friends he had not intended to come swimming, he is perfectly calm and does not grumble in the slightest. Indeed his strongest wish is to assert his independence.

> ' . . . if when in, I decide to practise a slight circular movement from right to left – or perhaps I should say,' he added, as he got into another eddy, 'from left to right, just as it happens to occur to me, it is nobody's business but my own.'

Critics who are both captious and superficial – generally the same with reference to our texts – may say Eeyore was guilty of some cognitive error when he asserted that his turning round and round in the water was what he had *decided* to do. The context strongly suggests that he was in fact being turned by eddies in the river.

To this objection there are two obvious answers. While he may not be turning by his independent muscular efforts, he is certainly allowing the movement and positively enjoying it. He is therefore perfectly justified in claiming that he has decided to practise ' a slight circular movement', first from right to left, then from left to right. Secondly, it is clear from his control of the situation that he has made a giant stride towards psychological health. Depression often results from feeling one is the helpless victim of circumstances or, worse still, of malignant enemies.

Eeyore's statement that he is one of those who can't experience gaiety or Bon-hommy is an example of the former; his comment that it was typical of 'Them' to take his tail exemplifies the latter. By now, Pooh has led Eeyore to see that both these attributions were cognitive errors. Pooh's own action in returning the tail and Christopher Robin's in restoring it to its proper place showed 'They' were not either hostile or indifferent. When Eeyore 'frisked about the forest, waving his tail so happily', and when he was 'as happy as could be' playing with the balloon and the Useful Pot, he must have learnt that he was capable of gaiety.

In both cases, his depression had been caused by misperception and the cure had begun by correcting this. A classic case of Cognitive Therapy.

We now come to one of those down-to-earth touches which confirm our confidence in the solid reality of the Milnean opus. While waiting for the delayed success of his scheme to land Eeyore by dropping a large stone which would wash his client ashore, 'Pooh was beginning to think that he must have chosen the wrong stone or the wrong river or the wrong day for his idea . . .'

Here Pooh himself is portrayed suffering anxiety and doubt concerning the rightness of his action. How are we to take this? Can we really believe that Pooh himself was wrong? How can we reconcile that belief with our often repeated principle that any apparent error must be in ourselves, not in Pooh?

The solution to that problem is clear to every reader who remembers that Pooh often *demonstrates* errors for the instruction of his pupils – and we are all his pupils. So far, so good. But what is the particular error he is demonstrating here? Confident that the solution will be in the text, we look back to the pages immediately preceding the description of Pooh's apparent anxiety.

When Rabbit asks,

'Eeyore, what are you doing there?' Eeyore answers, 'I'll give you three guesses, Rabbit. Digging holes in the ground? Wrong. Leaping from branch to branch of a young oak-tree? Wrong. Waiting for somebody to help me out of the river? Right.'

Though Eeyore states clearly that he wants to be helped out of the river, it becomes equally clear that he wants this in his own time and in his own way. He is not happy with the suggestion of dropping a stone near him. Moreover, the very last thing he says when Rabbit asks if he is ready for the stone, is a clear 'No'. Typically, Rabbit ignores this and tells Pooh to drop the stone.

To any truly wise psychologist, the answer now leaps from the page. Pooh is demonstrating the cardinal error of taking command instead of helping the *patient* to take control. This is a recurrent temptation to therapists of every sort, and indeed to all in what are called 'the caring professions'. All too often the laudable desire to help is contaminated with the itch to control. Here, as in every other respect, Winnie-the-Pooh is an example to all.

Having received and, I hope, heeded this warning to

professionals in the field, we next see how successfully Pooh heeded it himself. Far from meekly accepting a passive role, Eeyore asserts that, in order to avoid the stone dropped, "I dived and swam to the bank." When Pooh dropped the stone, he simply but effectively stimulated Eeyore to rescue himself.

## Eeyore's progress accelerates

From now on, we find rapidly accumulating evidence of his improving grasp of reality, that is, of the improving cognitive perception that Pooh was helping him to gain. When Piglet exclaims at his wetness, 'Eeyore shook himself, and asked somebody to explain to Piglet what happened when you had been inside a river for quite a long time.' Note his calm, factual explanation instead of the gloomy complaints he would have proffered before Pooh's application of Cognitive Therapy.

His new attitude is still more remarkably instanced when the cause of his fall into the river is discussed. When he has asserted that he was 'BOUNCED' into the river, Pooh asks him whether it was a joke or an accident. Instead of anger or bitterness, Eeyore responds with a cool analysis of his feelings, which must have rejoiced Pooh, both as a friend and as a therapist:

> 'I didn't stop to ask, Pooh. Even at the very bottom of the river I didn't stop to say to myself, "*Is* this a Hearty Joke, or is it the Merest Accident?" I just floated to the surface, and said to myself, 'It's wet'.'

Even when confronted with Tigger, Eeyore displays no more than a very moderate and understandable disapproval of Tigger's bounciness. He does not for a moment suggest that Tigger had any personal animus against him. He goes out of his way to say, 'I don't mind Tigger being in the Forest, because it's a large forest, and there's plenty of room to bounce in it.'

He objects only to Tigger's invading *his* little corner to bounce in *it*. Then he accepts Christopher Robin's tactful suggestion, "*I* think we all ought to play Poohsticks."

Finally, any suspicion that Eeyore's good humour was brief and superficial is dispelled when we read that, after the game, 'Tigger and Eeyore went off together, because Eeyore wanted to tell Tigger How to Win at Poohsticks, which you do by letting your stick drop in a twitchy sort of way, if you understand what I mean, Tigger . . .' This technical advice is particularly significant, because it shows not only a generalized good will but also an improved practical perception.

No wonder Pooh said, 'Everybody is *really* [all right]. That's what I think. But I don't suppose I'm right.' For a moment we may wonder whether Pooh's rather Panglossian optimism was the result of a brief euphoria, which he had to correct by his final comment. This is all right as far as it goes but it does not go far enough. I think his optimistic generalization applies to his friends in the Forest, while his more sceptical reservation shows him remembering that outer world where some inhabitants are beyond even his powers to heal. Christopher Robin's cheerful rejection of

Pooh's doubt is yet another example of good nature with limited understanding.

Eeyore's next appearance gives further evidence of his practical good will. Anxious to find a new home for Wol, whose 'old-world residence of great charm' had been destroyed by a storm, Eeyore unwittingly offers him Piglet's home. This potentially embarrassing mistake leads to a happy ending when Pooh invites Piglet to come and live with him.

Though Eeyore did fail to recognize Piglet's house, this was not, strictly speaking, a cognitive misperception. He did not recognize it presumably because he had not seen it before. And this was because he had confined himself too much to his own 'Gloomy Place'. In the circumstances, the truly significant fact is that Eeyore had left his accustomed solitude. And who had prompted this excursion? Rabbit, of course, after Pooh had channeled his Captainishness into the benevolent role of counsellor.

## Pooh's greatest therapeutic triumph

The crowning glory of Pooh's therapeutic career comes at the end of the opus, when it is the once reclusive, almost misanthropic, Eeyore who proposes the Rissolution in honour of Christopher Robin, who is about to leave the Forest for the outer world. More startling still, he reads his audience a poem of his own composition. At the end, he displays a truly professional approach: 'If anybody wants to clap, now is the time to do it' Equally professional is his reaction to their applause: 'Thank You. Unexpected and gratifying, if a little lacking in Smack.'

This remarkable event naturally calls for some commentary. Many enthusiastic admirers of the Great Bear have been puzzled, even shocked when they read Pooh's reaction to the poem: "It's much better than mine," said Pooh admiringly, and he really thought it was.' His spoken comment might be explained away either as audience politeness or as therapeutic encouragement. But neither of these can explain the authorial statement about his inward thoughts.

How can we reconcile this with the infallibility of Pooh's judgement? Some have suggested that Pooh, as so often, ahead of his time, was displaying a progressive admiration for the still revolutionary fashion for free verse. This is unconvincing. Even as free verse, the merit of Eeyore's POEM is debateable. Again, if Pooh really admired free verse, why did he not compose some of his own? The genuine answer must lie in Pooh's function as therapist. What was 'much better' in Eeyore's performance was his triumph over his previous inhibitions, a triumph due to Pooh's successful treatment. Pooh himself had never suffered from such problems, and therefore had no opportunity to triumph over them. In a literary sense, of course his poems were infinitely superior.

Though no Ursinologist can still puzzle over this little problem, some may understandably be pained by Eeyore's description of Pooh as 'a Bear with a Pleasing Manner but a Positively Startling Lack of Brain'. Does not this compound absurd misjudgement by gross ingratitude? As to the first, Pooh has cured Eeyore of his deep and long-standing depression. He has not endowed him with outstanding discrimination, though we may hope that such cognitive improvement may come later.

As for ingratitude, it is doubtful if Eeyore ever realized that his remarkable improvement was due to his ursine friend. No other therapist has worked as unobtrusively as Winnie-the-Pooh. Moreover, even when a therapist is recognized as such, cured patients are often more anxious to assert their independence than to acknowledge their debt to their healer. In a sense, this assertion may be the therapist's most convincing reward.

We may be confident that Pooh Bear knew all this and was quietly content with the knowledge of a Herculean task perfectly accomplished.

## Pooh's casebook: a retrospect

Winnie-the-Pooh's triumph in curing Eeyore's deep and long-standing depression is a fitting climax to this brief account of his therapeutic genius. The other examples I have selected show the variety of his cases and the uniformity of his success. As we progress through this casebook, we meet all Pooh's friends again and see him solve their problems. More than ever, we admire the literary tact with which Milne hinted at the complexities lying below the surface that has enchanted so many generations.

Pooh solves Wol's problem of communication. He leads the once timid Piglet to a proper self-esteem which finally enables him to display outstanding courage and generosity. He makes Tigger's bounciness socially acceptable without destroying his admirable vitality. He channels Rabbit's bossiness into the helpful role of a lay counsellor. The case of Kanga and Roo stands apart, for here we have a model of successful parenting. So Pooh has only to protect this happy mother and child from outside interference.

The very first case recorded here – Christopher Robin's phobia – may be less dramatic professionally, but it is perhaps even more important Ursinologically. If Pooh had not cured the irrational fear of bears (Arktophobia) that afflicted Christopher Robin in *When We Were Very Young* ('Lines and Squares'), the Pooh saga could never have even begun. To us as Ursinologists, could any other loss have equalled that? Could any cure have been more vital?

Like every work on Pooh, this book is inevitably selective. Once again, I can only hope that it will stimulate my readers to pursue their own researches, to widen and deepen their knowledge of Pooh as psychologist and psychotherapist.

Selective though it may be, this book does nevertheless show the breadth of Pooh's knowledge. Freudian numerology directs us to the psychological area of Pooh's Enormous Brain. On our way through our chosen case studies, we find Pooh applying Jungian typology, Adler's theory of the Inferiority Complex, Transactional Analysis, Behavioural Therapy, Gestalt Therapy and Cognitive Therapy. Experts in every one of those fields will doubtless marvel at the range of Pooh's knowledge – and at his judgement in applying it to particular cases. We must hope they will also take note of his technical innovations.

Perhaps even more important, Pooh himself suggests a solution to the most perplexing of all Ursinological problems: why has it taken so long for the Wisdom of Pooh to be recognized?

He provides this suggestion during Rabbit's misguided attempt to Unbounce Tigger. Readers will remember how Rabbit tries to lose Tigger in the Forest but instead gets lost himself together with his friends. When Pooh suggests his oblique method of finding the way home, Rabbit contemptuously dismisses it: 'I don't see much sense in that.'

'No,' said Pooh humbly, 'there isn't. But there was going to be when I began it. It's just that something happened to it on the way.'

Until very recently, we were all in Rabbit's condition. However warm our affection for Winnie-the-Pooh, we all too often responded to his wide knowledge and profound insights with 'I don't see much sense in that.' Pooh's own words tell us that he had begun to communicate sage advice and sound sense but 'something happened to it on the way'. What was this 'something' that so long blinded us to the Enormous Brain of Pooh?

As I suggested earlier, part of the answer lies in the very success of Pooh's appeal to children and, perhaps even more, to adults reading to children. Such an audience would hardly expect more than keen but unsophisticated enjoyment. And the surface meaning of the Pooh stories gives this superabundantly. We could hardly expect children to notice the underlying meanings, such as those I have explored in *Pooh and the Philosophers*, and *Pooh and the Ancient Mysteries*, and the psychological depths revealed in this little book. Many readers, when they have passed through the adolescent stage of despising their childhood pleasures, often look back to Pooh with nostalgic affection but rarely with intellectual alertness.

This explanation is true as far as it goes, but a knowledge of psychology can take us further. Because most of us first meet Winnie-the-Pooh when we are children, we naturally associate him with childish things. This connection is strengthened if we ourselves had much cherished teddy bears. The more affectionately we remembered him – and them – the more we were conditioned to accept him as a Bear of Very Little Brain.

According to the psychologist Dr Elizabeth Mapstone, a specialist in communication skills and negotation, we all tend to hear what we have learned to expect to hear. This kind of false hearing often leads to serious friction in personal relationships, as Dr Mapstone demonstrates in her *War of Words: Women and Men Arguing*. Similarly, the preconceived belief that the Milnean saga is only for children has led many devoted readers to accept Pooh as 'a Bear of Very Little Brain' and so remain deaf to his enormous wisdom. Dr Mapstone informs me that she is delighted to hear that her researches confirm the insights of Winnie-the-Pooh.

In recent years, devoted Ursinological scholars have revealed so many aspects of Pooh Bear's wisdom that there is now little excuse for continuing ignorance. I hope I have helped to dispel that ignorance by showing that the Pooh masterpieces contain the whole of Western philosophy and psychology and also prove that he is the Supreme Magus of the Second Millennium. *Pooh and the Psychologists* must be my last effort to reveal the Wisdom of Pooh. This is not, of course, because I would presume to set any limits to the Enormous Brain of Pooh, but because I must realistically acknowledge limits to my own.

I am happy in the hope that the revelation of Winnie-the-Pooh as a super-psychologist will both widen and deepen our appreciation of him and contribute to the happiness of the human species.

*The*
# Wisdom
*of*
# Pooh

## The prestigious list from Egmont

"The Wisdom of Pooh range proves beyond all reasonable doubt, what even Winnie-the-Pooh's most ardent fans may have hitherto underestimated, yet many will have long suspected; that indeed Pooh is a Bear of Enormous Brain."

**Titles inspired by the Stories of Winnie-the-Pooh
by A.A. Milne and illustrated by E.H. Shepard**

**The Tao of Pooh**
by Benjamin Hoff

**The Te of Piglet**
by Benjamin Hoff

**The Tao of Pooh & The Te of Piglet**
Combined Edition
by Benjamin Hoff

**Pooh and the Philosophers**
by John Tyerman Williams

**Pooh and the Second Millennium**
*A paperback edition of Pooh and the Ancient Mysteries*
by John Tyerman Williams

**Pooh and the Psychologists**
by John Tyerman Williams

**The Hums of Pooh**
by A.A. Milne

190

**Now We Are Seventy-five**
A selection of favourite stories and poems
in celebration of Pooh's 75th Anniversary

*Latin Editions*

**Winnie ille Pu**
by Alexander Lenard

**Domus Anguli Puensis**
by Brian Gerrard Staples

*Gift Editions*

*Winnie-the-Pooh's Little Books*

**Winnie-the-Pooh's Little Book of Wisdom**
**Eeyore's Little Book of Gloom**
**Tigger's Little Book of Bounce**
**Winnie-the-Pooh's Little Book of Feng Shui**

*Winnie-the-Pooh's Tiny Books*

**Wisdom from Pooh**
**Courage from Piglet**
**Thoughts from Eeyore**
**Cheer from Tigger**

*Winnie-the-Pooh's Little Valentines*

**Love from Pooh**
**Love From Piglet**

**Three Cheers for Pooh**
*A Celebration of the Best Bear in All the World*
by Brian Sibley

**NEW IN SEPTEMBER 2002**

**Say it Again, Pooh**
Collected thoughts of Winnie-the-Pooh
Compiled by Brian Sibley

*Also By John Tyerman Williams*
**Pooh and the Philosophers**
with line illustrations by E.H. Shepard

This witty and elegant *jeu d'esprit* sets out to prove beyond all reasonable doubt, that the whole of Western Philosophy, from the Cosmologists of Ancient Greece to the Existentialists of this century, may be found in *Winnie-the-Pooh* and *The House at Pooh Corner*. It shows how the Great Bear explains and illuminates the most profound ideas of the great thinkers, from Plato, Hume and Kant to Nietzsche, Heidegger and Sartre.

Even Winnnie-the-Pooh's most ardent fans may have hitherto underestimated his cosmic importance; this book will confirm, however, once and for all, what many will have long suspected: that Pooh is a Bear of Enormous Brain.

John Tyerman Williams is a Doctor of Philosophy and a former actor and lecturer on theatre, English history and English literature. He lives in Tintagel, Cornwall.

*Also By John Tyerman Williams*
**Pooh and the Second Millennium**
A paperback edition of Pooh and the Ancient
Mysteries with line illustrations by E.H. Shepard


*Pooh and the Second Millennium* reveals Winnie-the-Pooh as a
master of ancient lore and the supreme Magus of the Second
Millennium. John Tyerman Williams explores A.A. Milne's
classic stories *Winnie-the-Pooh* and *The House at Pooh Corner* to
reveal fascinating hidden references to the Millennium,
astrology, alchemy, hermetic philosophy, the Tarot, the
Druids, I Ching, the Qabalah and finally, the Female
Mysteries, which light the way to a Utopian society.

John Tyerman Williams proved in *Pooh and the Philosophers* that
the whole of Western philosophy may be found in the stories
of Winnie-the-Pooh. Now, he goes further to reveal the
hermetic tradition and the ancient mysteries of the world,
sealed inside a honey jar.

John Tyerman Williams is a Doctor of Philosophy and a
former actor and lecturer on theatre, English history and
English literature. He lives in Tintagel, Cornwall, close to the
birthplace of the Arthurian Legends.

**The Tao of Pooh**
by Benjamin Hoff
with line illustrations by E.H. Shepard

*The Tao of Pooh* has become a classic philosophical study of
Winnie-the-Pooh. Winnie-the-Pooh has a certain way about
him, a way of doing things which has made him the world's
most beloved bear. And Pooh's Way, as Benjamin Hoff
brilliantly demonstrates, seems strangely close to the ancient
Chinese principles of Taoism.

While Eeyore frets and Piglet hesitates, and Owl pontificates
... Pooh just *is*.

With examples from A.A. Milne's immensely popular
classics, *Winnie-the-Pooh* and *The House at Pooh Corner*, Benjamin
Hoff explains the principles of Taoist philosophy.

Benjamin Hoff is a writer, photographer, musician and
composer, and a specialist in Japanese fine-pruning, with a
degree in Asian Art. He writes full-time. In his spare time
he practises Taoist yoga and T'ai Chi Ch'uan. He lives in
Portland, Oregon.

*Also available in a combined paperback edition*
**The Tao of Pooh & The Te of Piglet**

**The Te of Piglet**
by Benjamin Hoff
with line illustrations by E.H. Shepard

In this sequel to *The Tao of Pooh*, author Benjamin Hoff explores the Te (a Chinese word meaning Virtue) — a principle embodied perfectly in Piglet. As delightful as it is instructive, *The Te of Piglet* features dialogues between the author and the familiar characters of Pooh, Eeyore, Tigger, Owl, Kanga and Baby Roo, and of course, Piglet himself. These conversations are interspersed with traditional Taoist stories and more than 50 illustrations by E.H. Shepard.

Combining the irresistible charm of A.A. Milne's classic stories, the enduring wisdom of the ancient teachings, and the unique contemporary appeal of its predecessor, *The Tao of Pooh*, Benjamin Hoff's second book, *The Te of Piglet*, is sure to captivate the legions of readers who have found enlightenment and pleasure in walking in the path of Pooh.

Benjamin Hoff is a writer, photographer, musician and composer, and a specialist in Japanese fine-pruning, with a degree in Asian Art. He writes full-time. In his spare time he practises Taoist yoga and T'ai Chi Ch'uan. He lives in Portland, Oregon.

*Also available in a combined paperback edition*
**The Tao of Pooh & The Te of Piglet**

# Winnie-the-Pooh's Little Books
with line illustrations by E.H. Shepard

### Winnie-the Pooh's Little Book of Wisdom
'Wise words from a Bear of Very Little Brain'
A honey pot full of Wise Words and Useful advice on the
Problems and Pleasures of life.

### Eeyore's Little Book of Gloom
'Read this book  - then you'll be sorry . . .'
A leaden collection of Pessimistic Ponderings from the
Hundred Acre Wood's resident cynic. Perfect for those who are
tired of Life or tedious little Tomes full of joy.

### Tigger's Little Book of Bounce
'Tiggers can do anything – and so can you!'
A little book bursting with Bouncy Bon Mots about Things
Tiggers like – and Kanga's and Pooh's as well, but not Eeyores.
It's *The* Guide to Get-Up-and-Go!

### Winnie-the-Pooh's  Little Book of Feng Shui
'When feng shui came to the Forest . . .'

Winnie-the-Pooh might not know it, but feng shui is about
what Bears do Best – living in harmony with their
surroundings. A little book filled with feng shui tips from
Pooh and his friends, on how to bring greater harmony into
*your* life.

*Winnie-the-Pooh's Tiny Books*
with line illustrations by E.H. Shepard

Wisdom from Pooh
Courage from Piglet
Thoughts from Eeyore
Cheer from Tigger

Four delightful tiny format books which are just the right size for little gifts for furry paws. Each little book dips into the World of Pooh and his friends with selected quotations from *Winnie-the-Pooh* and *The House at Pooh Corner.*

From Pooh are found words of Wisdom about Life, which are as relevant today as they were seventy-five years ago. It is hard to be Brave when you are Only Small, but Piglet's courage grows as he finds that he is brave after all. Eeyore imparts his thoughts both gloomy and hopeful on life and its problems, while Tigger brings cheer with his bouncy optimism.

## Now We Are Seventy-five
Selected from the Stories and Poems by A.A. Milne
with line illustrations by E.H. Shepard

By way of celebration, for his seventy-fifth anniversary, Pooh
put together a Special Selection of his favourite stories and
poems from *Winnie-the-Pooh, The House at Pooh Corner, When We Were
Very Young* and *Now We Are Six.*

With text by A.A.Milne and line illustrations by E.H. Shepard,
Now We Are Seventy-five is a Little Smackerel of Something
about a Very Important Bear.

# The Hums of Pooh
By A.A. Milne
with line illustrations by E.H. Shepard

Pooh makes up Hums for all sorts of occasions. Hums are Pooh's way of thinking about his friends, or honey or the weather. "It isn't Brain, because You Know Why, but it just comes to me sometimes," says Pooh.

*The Hums of Pooh* from *Winnie-the-Pooh* and *The House at Pooh Corner* with an explanation by A. A. Milne to each of the Hums are accompanied by illustrations by E. H. Shepard.

**Three Cheers for Pooh**
A Celebration of the Best Bear in All the World
by Brian Sibley
with colour and line illustrations by E.H. Shepard
and full colour and black and white photographs.

Winnie-the-Pooh, introduced to us in 1926 by A.A.Milne, has
become a worldwide celebrity. Winnie-the-Pooh, the Bear of
remarkable literary fame is introduced to us again, seventy-five
years later, by Brian Sibley as he sets out to tell us Just What
Pooh *"did"*.

From Christopher Robin's beloved teddy bear, to the Bear now
known and loved by children the world over, Brian Sibley
explores how Pooh got his name, how A.A.Milne came to write
the stories found in *Winnie-the-Pooh* and *The House at Pooh Corner*,
and how with the help of E.H.Shepard's endearing illustrations
of Pooh, Christopher Robin and his Bear "will always be
playing".